20th Anniversary Edition
THE SPIRIT OF CHRISTMAS

CREATIVE HOLIDAY IDEAS

The years flow quickly past us in this busy age. That's why it's nice to know we can rely on the traditions of Christmas to capture our special memories of the season. As you turn the pages of this 20th anniversary edition of The Spirit of Christmas, *take a little time to reminisce with us over treasured ornaments and flavorful recipes from the past. Once you've enjoyed the sights and flavors of holidays gone by, you'll also find plenty of original ideas for dazzling decorations, glorious gifts, and delicious dishes. This year, blend the best of the old with the brightest of the new—the memories you create will shine for all the years to come.*

LEISURE ARTS, INC.
Little Rock, Arkansas

CONTENTS

Celebrating 20 Years of The Spirit of Christmas 4

Celebrating 20 Years of Sights 6

Celebrating 20 Years of Tastes 12

The Sights of Christmas 20

It's a Wonderful Life 22

Snow News 30

A Beach House Christmas 36

Whimsical Christmas 46

Icy Splendor 52

Glitter & Glitz 60

The Sharing of Christmas 68

Under the Tree 70

Gifts for Every Taste 74

The Tastes of Christmas 82

Dinner at the Mansion 84

Christmas Cookery 101 92

Sweet Christmas Celebration 100

Southwestern Grill Out 108

Project Instructions 116

Patterns 159

General Instructions 185

Project Index 188

Recipe Index 190

Credits 192

"... and it was always said of him, that he knew how to keep Christmas well, if any man alive possessed the knowledge. May that be truly said of us, and all of us!"

— From *A Christmas Carol* by Charles Dickens

067243

The Spirit of Christmas—
Remembering 20 Years

"...and it was always said of him, that he knew how to keep Christmas well..."

Since 1987, the epigraph for each edition of *The Spirit of Christmas* has been this timeless quote from Charles Dickens' *A Christmas Carol*. In the classic holiday tale, a fictional curmudgeon learns that everlasting life and joy are his to keep if only he will welcome the spirit of Christmas into his heart.

At Leisure Arts, we know that everyone can benefit from a little more joy, especially during the busy Christmas season. It is our hope that your heart has welcomed the creative spirit we have shared in our ideas for holiday gifts, recipes, and decorations.

Working on this twentieth edition of *The Spirit of Christmas* has renewed many fond memories for our staff, including the first brainstorming session for Book One. Back then, the Leisure Arts editorial staff crowded around a tiny lunchroom table to discuss the challenge set before us: Could we produce an annual holiday idea book that would bring you the year's best ideas for stylish decorations, unforgettable gifts, and mouth-watering foods?

Everyone in that small lunchroom had positive feelings about our assorted strengths and talents. That optimism served us well as we set to work. We sent our designers to markets around the country to discover the latest trends for each year, and our book sales blossomed as Christmas fans found exciting new ideas that inspired their creativity.

As the staff of Leisure Arts reminisces about this much-loved book series, we want to thank you, dear reader, for making us a part of your Yuletide celebrations through the years. We hope that your Christmases—past, present, and future—are brighter, merrier, and more memorable because of *The Spirit of Christmas*. And may you always hold within your heart the desire to "keep Christmas well."

Celebrating Lights

2006
book twenty

This quick-to-make
Keepsake Ornament will add
plenty of glitz to your tree.

Adding a keepsake ornament to the tree each year is a favorite holiday tradition for many of us. In the 20 years we've been publishing *The Spirit of Christmas*, we've presented hundreds of wonderful tree trims from which our readers could choose. Here's a look back at the ornaments that were best-loved by our editors.

Instructions for Celebrating 20 Years of Sights *begin on page 116.*

The Beribboned Ornament is another quick project that satisfies the need for originality.

2005

book nineteen

Sparkling beads look like elegant jewels on this Snowflake Pillow Ornament.

2004

book eighteen

Lovely to look at, yet sturdier than many other kinds of decorations, a Wood Burned Star will last forever.

2003

book seventeen

A Frosted Ball with Beaded Collar shows how an ordinary ornament can become an heirloom.

2002

book sixteen

Easy stitches will make your fingers fly to create an entire flock of Embroidered Bird Ornaments.

2001

book fifteen

Simple sewing and dazzling beadwork create a Love Pillow Ornament that also makes a thoughtful gift.

2000

book fourteen

Unless you plan to make extras, don't let your friends see your finished Joy Redwork Ornament!

1999

book thirteen

Woven with silver ribbon, this Crocheted Angel will add a glow to your tree for many years to come.

1998

book twelve

Use tissue paper and other simple supplies to portray the Madonna and Child in simulated stained glass.

 *1997*

book eleven

Honor a heavenly guardian by creating a radiant Poinsettia Angel for your tree.

 *1996*

book ten

The traditional design of this Folk-Art Appliquéd Ornament uses just three easy embroidery stitches.

 *1995*

book nine

Make a Crocheted Snowflake whenever you have a few minutes to spare, and you'll soon have a flurry of the wintry decorations.

 *1994*

book eight

What could be more fun than a Penguin on skis? Perhaps a whole tree filled with his Antarctic pals in painted papier-mâché!

1993
book seven

Who's the snazzy dresser? It's a friendly Santa Ornament, looking resplendent in sequins.

1992
book six

Classic cross stitch captures this angel in flight. The seraphim trumpets Glory to God in celebration of Christmas.

1991
book five

Or was it 1890? This Hanging Tin Star hearkens back to the days when trees were trimmed with candles, fruit, and rustic shapes.

1990
book four

The needlepoint Santa Door Hanger greets holiday guests with old-fashioned charm.

1989
book three

Difficult to pronounce but easy to love, this Scherenschnitte Reindeer may leap into your heart and become your favorite decoration.

1988
book two

Since so many of our designs first came to life on paper, it seems right that this nostalgic look back should end with a little Scherenschnitte Tree.

1987
book one

These ornaments from the past are all lovely reminders that the spirit of Christmas moves from the heart to the hand, before returning to the heart again!

Instructions for Celebrating 20 Years of Sights begin on page 116.

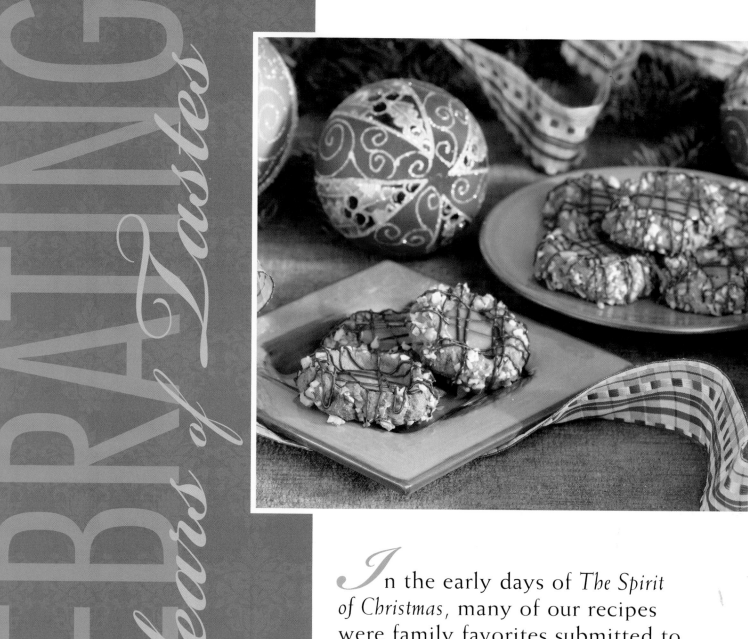

CELEBRATING
20 Years of Lasting Tastes

*I*n the early days of *The Spirit of Christmas*, many of our recipes were family favorites submitted to the test kitchen by employees. As the years went by, the process was often reversed as staff members began serving our new dishes at home. We thought it would be fun in this anniversary edition to share past recipes that have become top choices with our toughest critics— our families.

CHOCOLATE-CARAMEL THUMBPRINTS

Laura Holyfield, Craft Production Writer, shares a story about these cookies from 2004. "Last year we had an ice storm just before Christmas. I had the best time making several different batches of cookies to give to my neighbors. I tried these cookies for the first time. They were so festive and delicious. Everyone enjoyed them, especially the baker. (I had to make sure they tasted all right!)"

- ³/₄ cup butter or margarine, softened
- ¹/₂ cup sugar
- 2 squares (1 ounce each) semisweet baking chocolate, melted
- 1 egg yolk
- 2 teaspoons vanilla extract
- 1¹/₂ cups all-purpose flour
- ¹/₄ teaspoon baking soda
- ¹/₂ teaspoon salt
- ³/₄ cup very finely chopped pecans
- 16 caramels
- 2¹/₂ tablespoons whipping cream
- ²/₃ cup semisweet chocolate morsels
- 2 teaspoons shortening

Beat butter at medium speed with an electric mixer until creamy; gradually add sugar, beating well. Add melted chocolate and egg yolk, beating until blended. Stir in vanilla. Combine flour, baking soda, and salt; add to butter mixture, beating well.

Shape dough into 1-inch balls; roll balls in chopped pecans. Place balls 1 inch apart on greased cookie sheets. Press thumb gently into center of each ball, leaving an indentation. Bake at 350° for 12 minutes or until set.

Meanwhile, combine caramels and whipping cream in top of a double boiler over simmering water. Cook over medium-low heat, stirring constantly, until caramels melt and mixture is smooth. Remove cookies from oven, cool slightly, and press center of each cookie again. Quickly spoon ³/₄ teaspoon caramel mixture into center of each cookie. Remove cookies to wire racks to cool.

Place chocolate morsels and shortening in a 1-quart zip-top freezer bag; seal bag. Microwave on HIGH 1 to 1¹/₂ minutes; squeeze bag until chocolate melts. Snip a tiny hole in one corner of bag, using scissors. Drizzle chocolate over cooled cookies.

Yield: about 2¹/₂ dozen cookies

CHOCOLATE ESPRESSO CHEESECAKE

Susan Johnson, Senior Editorial Writer, remembers haunting the break area after this fudgey 2002 indulgence was photographed, just hoping for another taste! She says, "Don't fool yourself that a small slice of this cheesecake will be enough."

- 2¹/₂ cups graham cracker crumbs
- ¹/₂ cup plus 2 tablespoons butter or margarine, melted
- 2 teaspoons almond extract
- 4 packages (8 ounces each) cream cheese, softened
- ²/₃ cup sugar
- 3 large eggs
- 8 squares (1 ounce each) semisweet baking chocolate, melted
- ¹/₃ cup milk
- 2 teaspoons instant espresso powder
- Garnish: chocolate curls

In a medium bowl, combine cracker crumbs, butter, and almond extract; stir well. Press mixture on bottom and 2 inches up sides of a 9-inch springform pan. Set aside.

Preheat oven to 350°. In a mixing bowl, beat cream cheese at high speed with an electric mixer until creamy. Gradually add sugar, beating well. Add eggs, 1 at a time, beating well after each addition. Add melted chocolate; beat well. Combine milk and espresso powder, stirring until powder dissolves. Add to cream cheese mixture; beat until smooth. Pour mixture into prepared crust.

Bake 45 to 50 minutes or until center is almost set. Let cool to room temperature in pan on a wire rack; cover and chill 8 hours. Carefully remove sides of springform pan. Garnish, if desired.

Yield: about 12 servings

Pour mixture through a strainer into a 13 x 9-inch glass baking dish. Place dish in a large baking pan. Add water to larger pan to come halfway up sides of baking dish. Bake 1 to 1½ hours or until knife inserted in center comes out clean. Cool to room temperature. Cover with plastic wrap and refrigerate 6 to 8 hours.

Set oven on broil. Pat top of dessert with paper towel to remove excess moisture. Cover top evenly with remaining ½ cup brown sugar. Place dessert under broiler just until sugar begins to melt, about 5 minutes. Watch dessert carefully as the sugar will melt very quickly.

For sweetened whipped cream, beat all ingredients in a large bowl at high speed with an electric mixer until soft peaks form.

Serve brûlée warm or chilled with a dollop of sweetened whipped cream.

Yield: 12 to 15 servings

CHOCOLATE CRÈME BRÛLÉE

Susan Wiles, Special Projects Director, remembers sitting in the former Maison Louis Restaurant while the Leisure Arts Food Editor tried to figure out the ingredients for this brûlée. In 1988, restaurant owner Louis Petit shared his wonderful recipe with us.

Brûlée
- 1 quart whipping cream
- 1 cup firmly packed brown sugar, divided
- 2 tablespoons granulated sugar
- 8 ounces premium quality milk chocolate, chopped
- 7 egg yolks
- 1 teaspoon vanilla extract

Sweetened Whipped Cream
- 1 cup whipping cream
- ½ cup granulated sugar
- 1½ teaspoons vanilla extract

For brûlée, preheat oven to 350°. In a heavy saucepan over medium-high heat, bring cream, ½ cup brown sugar, and granulated sugar to a boil. Add chocolate and remove from heat; stir until chocolate melts. Allow to cool slightly.

In a medium bowl, whisk egg yolks and vanilla until blended. Whisk ¼ cup chocolate mixture into eggs. Pour in remaining chocolate mixture and whisk until blended.

BROWNIE-MINT PIE

Cyndi Hansen, Senior Design Director, likes this 2003 recipe because it's easy to prepare and everyone loves it. She makes brownies all year, but saves this pie for special occasions.

- 1 package (4.6 ounces) chocolate mints
- 1 package (15.8 ounces) brownie mix and ingredients to prepare brownies
- 1 unbaked (9-inch) deep-dish frozen piecrust, thawed
  Vanilla ice cream
  Hot fudge topping

Use a vegetable peeler to shave 3 tablespoons mint curls for serving; set aside. Chop remaining mints. Prepare brownie mix according to package directions. Stir in chopped mints. Pour into piecrust. Bake at 350° for 45 minutes or until done; cool slightly. Serve with ice cream, hot fudge topping, and reserved mint curls.

Yield: one 9-inch pie

For filling, peel and quarter 2 oranges. Quarter remaining unpeeled orange. Process oranges in a large food processor until coarsely chopped. Add apples; process until fruit is finely chopped. Transfer fruit to a large bowl and stir in sugar. Add liqueur, if desired. Spread about 1 cup filling between each layer. Press remaining filling over top and sides of cake. Cover and chill 3 hours before serving.

Yield: 12 to 14 servings

SUGAR-AND-SPICE PECANS

Office Manager Carol Mulach has always found this 2002 recipe to be a welcomed gift. When Carol's daughter moved out of state, she requested the recipe so she could make gifts for her new co-workers. Her daughter's gift list grows each year, because more and more people look forward to these pecans at Christmas.

- ³/₄ cup sugar
- 1 teaspoon ground cinnamon
- ¹/₂ teaspoon salt
- ¹/₄ teaspoon ground nutmeg
- ¹/₄ teaspoon ground allspice
- ¹/₄ teaspoon ground cloves
- 1 egg white
- 2¹/₂ tablespoons water
- 8 cups pecan halves

In a medium bowl, combine sugar, cinnamon, salt, nutmeg, allspice, cloves, egg white, and water; stir well. Add pecans; stir until evenly coated. Spread in a lightly greased, aluminum foil-lined 15¹/₂ x 10¹/₂-inch jellyroll pan. Bake at 275° for 50 to 55 minutes, stirring occasionally.

Remove from pan and cool on waxed paper. Store pecans in an airtight container.

Yield: about 8 cups pecans

FRESH APPLE AND ORANGE CAKE

Nora Faye Taylor, former Test Kitchen Assistant, has many favorites, but this recipe is closest to her heart. It was featured in the 1998 edition but originally came from her ninety-six-year-old mother, Etta Mae Spencer. During World War II, when sugar was rationed, Mrs. Spencer made this cake using a Christmas gift of apples and oranges from her husband's employer. It became her husband's favorite dessert. Nora Faye still makes this cake every Christmas.

Cake

- ¹/₂ cup butter or margarine, softened
- 1³/₄ cups sugar
- 2 eggs
- 1¹/₂ teaspoons vanilla extract
- 2³/₄ cups all-purpose flour
- 2¹/₂ teaspoons baking powder
- ¹/₂ teaspoon salt
- 1¹/₄ cups milk

Filling

- 3 navel oranges
- 3 unpeeled apples, cored and quartered
- 1¹/₄ cups sugar
- 2 tablespoons orange-flavored liqueur (optional)

For cake, grease three 8-inch round cake pans and line bottoms with waxed paper. In a large bowl, cream butter and sugar until fluffy. Add eggs and vanilla; beat until smooth. In a medium bowl, combine flour, baking powder, and salt. Alternately add dry ingredients and milk to creamed mixture; beat until well blended. Pour batter into prepared pans. Bake in a 350° oven for 23 to 28 minutes or until a toothpick inserted in center of cake comes out clean. Cool in pans 10 minutes. Remove from pans and cool completely on a wire rack.

SHERRIED FRUIT COBBLER

This 1991 recipe was chosen by Sandra Case, Vice President and Editor-in-Chief, as her favorite. It's also popular with many other staff members.

Cobbler

1 can (15½ ounces) sliced pineapple, drained
1 can (16 ounces) peach halves, drained
1 can (16 ounces) pear halves, drained
1 can (16 ounces) apricot halves, drained
1 jar (6 ounces) maraschino cherries, drained
1 can (21 ounces) apple pie filling
½ cup butter
2 tablespoons all-purpose flour
1 teaspoon ground cinnamon
½ teaspoon ground nutmeg
¼ teaspoon ground allspice
½ cup firmly packed brown sugar
1 cup cooking sherry

Topping

¼ cup butter
1 cup graham cracker crumbs

For cobbler, arrange drained fruit and pie filling in a 3-quart baking dish. Melt butter in a medium saucepan over low heat. Stir in next 5 ingredients. Slowly add sherry, stirring constantly; cook over medium heat until thickened. Pour over fruit. Cover and chill 8 hours or overnight.

Allow cobbler to come to room temperature. Bake in a 350° oven for 20 to 25 minutes or until bubbly.

For topping, melt butter in a small saucepan and stir in graham cracker crumbs. Spread crumbs evenly over cobbler and bake 5 minutes longer until crumbs are browned.

Yield: about 10 servings

CARAMEL GRAHAM CRACKERS

Several people named this 1987 recipe their favorite. Gloria Bearden, former Creative Director, and Leslie Dunn, former Test Kitchen Assistant, are among those who gave it high marks. These tasty cookies are easy to make.

24 cinnamon graham crackers
    (2½-inch square each)
½ cup margarine
½ cup butter
1 cup firmly packed
    brown sugar
1 cup chopped pecans

Line a 15½ x 10½ x 1-inch baking pan with aluminum foil; cover with single layer of graham crackers.

Mix margarine, butter, and brown sugar in a saucepan; bring to a boil and cook for 2 minutes. Pour mixture over crackers; sprinkle pecans on top. Bake in a 350° oven for 12 minutes. Cut into triangles while warm.

Yield: about 4 dozen crackers

POLYNESIAN MEATBALLS

"This is one of the recipes we published in 1991 when I was on the testing team," says Sherry O'Connor, former Managing Editor. "It was a really good recipe, but my husband, Michael, and I were completely surprised when we served it at a party. Everyone stood around the slow cooker all evening until it was all gone! Though it is a little more time-intensive than some party fare, it never fails to get rave reviews."

Meatballs

1½ pounds ground pork
1¼ pounds ground round
2 cups crushed corn flake cereal
2 eggs, beaten
1 cup milk
3 tablespoons prepared horseradish
3 tablespoons Worcestershire sauce
2 teaspoons dry mustard
1 teaspoon salt
½ teaspoon ground black pepper

Sauce

1 cup ketchup
½ cup firmly packed brown sugar
½ cup water
⅓ cup soy sauce
2 tablespoons honey
2 tablespoons apple cider vinegar
1 teaspoon dry mustard
1 can (8 ounces) crushed pineapple, drained

For meatballs, combine all ingredients in a large bowl, mixing well. Shape mixture into 1-inch balls. Place on a rack in a shallow baking pan. Bake at 450° for 12 to 15 minutes or until browned; drain.

For sauce, combine all ingredients except pineapple in a large saucepan over medium-high heat. Bring to a boil; reduce heat to medium and simmer 10 minutes. Stir in pineapple. Spoon meatballs into sauce, stirring until well coated. Continue to cook 10 to 15 minutes or until heated through. Serve hot.

Yield: about 75 meatballs

SWEET OR SAVORY PASTRIES

Cheryl Gunnells, Executive Director of Publications, rates this 2000 recipe as her all-time favorite. These pastries may be assembled ahead of time and chilled until ready to bake, making them perfect for Cheryl's busy schedule.

Ham and Cheese

- 1 sheet (from a 17.3-ounce package) frozen puff pastry, thawed according to package directions
- 4 ounces cream cheese, softened
- 1 egg
- 1 tablespoon chopped green onion
- 2 teaspoons prepared mustard
- 1 cup shredded sharp Cheddar cheese
- 4 ounces shaved ham

Lemon-Almond

- 1 sheet (from a 17.3-ounce package) frozen puff pastry, thawed according to package directions
- 1 package (8 ounces) cream cheese, softened
- 1/3 cup powdered sugar
- 1 tablespoon freshly-squeezed lemon juice
- 1 teaspoon grated lemon zest
- 1 teaspoon almond extract
- 3/4 cup sliced almonds, toasted

Preheat oven to 375°. For ham and cheese pastry, place pastry sheet between sheets of plastic wrap and roll into a 10 x 15-inch rectangle. Use plastic wrap to transfer dough to a nonstick 14 x 17-inch baking sheet; remove plastic wrap.

Beat cream cheese, egg, onion, and mustard in a medium bowl until fluffy. Stir in cheese. Spread cheese mixture over pastry to within 3 inches of long edges. Place ham over cheese mixture. Use a knife to make 2-inch-long cuts 1 inch apart along long edges (**Fig. 1**).

Fig. 1

Fig. 2

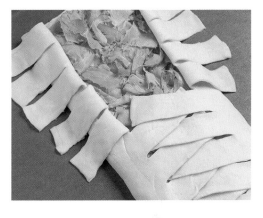

Beginning at one short edge and alternating sides, fold pastry strips over filling (**Fig. 2**).

Bake 28 to 30 minutes or until golden brown. Cool in pan 15 minutes. Serve warm or at room temperature.

For lemon-almond pastry, follow ham and cheese instructions to roll out pastry. Beat cream cheese, powdered sugar, lemon juice, lemon zest, and almond extract in a medium bowl until fluffy. Spread cream cheese mixture over pastry to within 3 inches of long edges. Sprinkle almonds over cream cheese mixture. Continue to follow ham and cheese instructions to cut and fold dough strips and to bake pastry.

Yield: about 10 slices each pastry

Bacon-Cheese Ring

Pam Warren, former Production Writer, brought this 1988 recipe to a potluck where it became an instant success. She called it Catch-a-Man Dip because it was so popular with men.

- 1 package (12 ounces) bacon, cooked and crumbled
- 1 pound extra-sharp Cheddar cheese, shredded
- 1 bunch green onions, finely chopped
- 2 cups mayonnaise
- 1 teaspoon cayenne pepper
- 1/2 cup toasted, slivered almonds
  Strawberry preserves
  Crackers or French bread to serve

Combine bacon, cheese, green onions, mayonnaise, and cayenne pepper in a medium bowl. Place almonds in the bottom of an oiled 7-cup ring mold; press cheese mixture into mold. Refrigerate overnight.

Unmold cheese ring into serving dish. Place a small custard cup filled with strawberry preserves in center of ring. Serve with crackers or French bread slices.
Yield: 20 to 25 servings

Onion Casserole

Mary Hutcheson, Special Projects Editor, joined Leisure Arts the same year this casserole was developed. The 1991 recipe won her favor the first time she cooked Thanksgiving dinner for her family.

- 2 large yellow onions, thinly sliced and separated into rings, divided
- 2 large red onions, thinly sliced and separated into rings, divided
- 12 green onions, chopped and divided
- 1 teaspoon ground black pepper, divided
- 10 ounces bleu cheese, crumbled
- 10 ounces (about 2 1/2 cups) shredded Havarti cheese
- 3 tablespoons butter or margarine, cut into small pieces
- 3/4 cup dry white wine

In a greased 9 x 13-inch baking dish, layer one-half of yellow, red, and green onions. Sprinkle 1/2 teaspoon pepper over onions. Top with bleu cheese. Layer remaining onions and sprinkle remaining 1/2 teaspoon pepper over top. Top with Havarti cheese. Place butter evenly over cheese. Pour wine over casserole. Bake at 350° for 1 hour or until onions are tender. If cheese browns too quickly, cover with aluminum foil. Serve hot.
Yield: about 12 servings
Note: Casserole may be assembled 1 day in advance and refrigerated. Increase baking time to 1 hour and 15 minutes.

MEXICAN ROLLED MEAT LOAF

The wonderful aroma of this 1998 entrée traveled from the test kitchen to the office of Jennifer Hutchings, Craft Production Writer—on the other side of the building! She said that when she tasted it, she was so impressed with the flavor that she went home and made it for her family. They agreed that this one was a winner!

     2 tablespoons vegetable oil
   1/2 cup chopped onion
   1/2 cup chopped celery
   1/4 cup chopped red bell pepper
   1/4 cup chopped green bell pepper
     2 tablespoons chopped yellow
         bell pepper
     4 garlic cloves, minced
   1/2 cup drained whole kernel
         yellow corn
   1/2 cup chopped fresh cilantro
     1 pound lean ground beef
     1 pound lean breakfast sausage
  1 1/4 cups salsa, divided
   3/4 cup plain bread crumbs
     2 eggs
  1 1/2 teaspoons ground cumin
     1 teaspoon chili powder
   1/2 teaspoon salt
   1/2 teaspoon ground black pepper
     2 cups (8 ounces) shredded
         Monterey Jack cheese,
         divided
       Garnish: fresh cilantro

In a medium skillet, heat oil over medium-high heat. Add onion, celery, bell peppers, and garlic. Stirring constantly, cook about 10 minutes or until vegetables are tender. Stir in corn and chopped cilantro; set aside.

In a large bowl, combine beef, sausage, 1/2 cup salsa, bread crumbs, eggs, cumin, chili powder, salt, and black pepper. Press meat mixture into a 10 x 14-inch rectangle on a piece of plastic wrap. Spread vegetable mixture over meat mixture to within 1 inch of edges. Sprinkle with 1 cup cheese. Beginning at 1 long edge and using plastic wrap to hold shape, roll up meat mixture jellyroll style; press to seal edge and ends. Transfer roll, seam side down,

to a 15 1/2 x 10 1/2-inch jellyroll pan. Remove plastic wrap. Bake in a 350° oven for 50 to 55 minutes or until juices run clear. Cool 30 minutes in pan. Remove from pan; cover and chill 4 hours or overnight.

To serve, cut meat loaf into 1-inch slices. Arrange slices on a heatproof serving dish. Spoon remaining 3/4 cup salsa over slices. Cover with aluminum foil and bake in a 300° oven for 30 minutes. Uncover and sprinkle remaining 1 cup cheese over top; bake 5 minutes longer or until cheese slightly melts. Garnish, if desired.
Yield: about 12 servings

BUFFET BURGERS

"Ever since they appeared in the 1998 edition, these mini burgers have become a must-have appetizer at my house for New Year's Day football watching," says Kathy Elrod, Concept Designer.

     2 pounds lean ground beef
   1/2 cup chopped onion
     1 cup soft bread crumbs
     1 egg, lightly beaten
     1 tablespoon mayonnaise
     1 teaspoon garlic salt
     1 teaspoon Italian seasoning
   1/4 teaspoon freshly ground black
         pepper
  1 1/2 cups shredded mozzarella
         cheese
    20 small, square rolls, heated and
         cut in half
       Mustard and mayonnaise to serve

Combine beef, onion, bread crumbs, egg, mayonnaise, and seasonings; mix well. Keeping meat mixture one inch from edges, press mixture into bottom of a 15 1/2 x 10 1/2-inch jellyroll pan. Bake at 350° for 20 to 25 minutes; drain. Top meat with cheese and bake 5 to 8 minutes longer or until cheese melts. Remove from oven and let stand about 5 minutes. Cut into 20 squares and place in rolls. Serve with mustard and mayonnaise.
Yield: 20 appetizer-size burgers

FREEZER MARGARITAS

Rhonda Shelby, Art Publications Director, didn't have to be asked twice for her favorite recipe! This delicious beverage appeared in the 1998 edition.

     2 cups water
     1 cup sugar
  1 1/2 cups freshly-squeezed lime juice
         (about 8 limes)
  1 1/2 cups tequila
   3/4 cup Triple Sec liqueur
       Garnish: lime rind curls

In a small saucepan, combine water and sugar over high heat. Stirring frequently, bring mixture to a boil. Remove syrup from heat and cool 1 hour.

In a 2-quart freezer container, combine syrup, lime juice, tequila, and liqueur. Cover and freeze overnight.

To serve, spoon into glasses and garnish, if desired.
Yield: about 6 1/2 cups margaritas

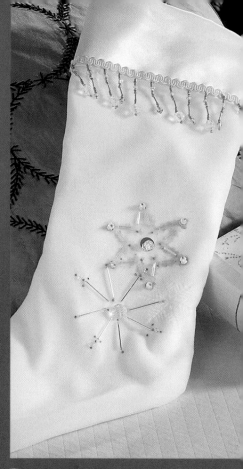

THE SIGHTS

OF CHRISTMAS

This Christmas, come home to a cozy beach house filled with the romance of the sea. Or let a comical Santa preside over your whimsical Yuletide. Whether you wish for the warmth of red riches or delight in the wintry magic of silver and white, you'll find these wondrous things and more in the following pages. Even your New Year will shine brighter in our merry, metallic hues. Let these visions of seasonal décor inspire you to create the most memorable holiday of all—the Christmas of your dreams.

It's A Wonderful Life

Christmas is
a season of celebration!
It's a time for family and
friends to come together
and rejoice. It's also an
occasion to enjoy favorite
Yuletide traditions while
creating new ones. This
rich setting, with its
nostalgic decorations,
is the ideal backdrop for
holiday gatherings you'll
always remember.

Instructions for It's a Wonderful Life begin on page 124.

*B*eckon guests to join your seasonal celebrations by topping an entryway with a **Glittered Swag**. Little decorative touches sprinkled throughout your home—such as **Crewel Cropped Stockings**, a rosy **Hanging Basket Arrangement**, a unique **Button Pillow**, and a **Crewel Pillow**—really add festive flair!

Instructions for It's a Wonderful Life begin on page 124.

Create a backdrop for a joyous celebration by adorning your Christmas tree with this dazzling **Glittered Garland**. A timeless **Crewel Tree Skirt** will provide a graceful foundation for your evergreen, as well as your Yuletide offerings.

*H*ave you been looking for a clever way to display your collection of vintage Christmas cards? Simply transform them into **Framed Ornaments**! **Flocked and Matte Red Glass Balls** trim the tree with a traditional touch.

*U*se your scrapbooking supplies to dress up your holiday gifts. A collection of **Layered Packages** will have everyone wondering what treasures nestle within the "timeworn" wrappings.

Instructions for It's a Wonderful Life *begin on page 124.*

*S*et a sophisticated tone with a velvety **Table Skirt** and a classic **Crewel Topper**. A **Rose Arrangement** is the table's crowning touch, while a **Ribbon Pillow** adds color and comfort to a side chair. For memorable accents, craft **Framed Pieces** using family photos, holiday postcards, and scrapbook embellishments.

Instructions for It's a Wonderful Life begin on page 124.

SnowNews

*H*ave you heard the latest? Snow is in the forecast for Christmas—no matter where you live! This artsy assortment of snow-inspired projects, many of which are made from newspaper, will blanket your home in snowy splendor.

Instructions for Snow News *begin on page 128.*

*T*his dapper **Snow Fellow** is so darling, it's "snow" wonder you can't help falling in love with him!

$\mathcal{M}$ake your tree look as though it's covered in snow by trimming it with an assortment of frosty baubles. On this page, clockwise from top left, are a **Snowflake Tree Topper**, Tin Star Ornament, **Stamped Twill Garland**, Glittery Cardstock Snowflake, **Papier-Mâché Snowball**, Snowflake Garland, and bright red **Finger Chain Garland**.

Instructions for Snow News *begin on page 128.*

$\mathcal{A}$dd more cheer to your tree with these three wintry decorations (*left, top to bottom*): a Snowman Ornament, Glittery Newsprint Snowflake, and Stamped Snowflake Spangle. To construct a quick, charming tree stand, simply use a galvanized bucket. Carry out the newsworthy theme by fashioning a tree skirt from crumpled newspaper.

$\mathcal{E}$ven if the weather doesn't cooperate, you can have a white Christmas when you decorate the tree with a flurry of unique, hand-crafted trims.

$\mathcal{T}$ry something new this year—use rubber boots as stockings! Set them by the tree and fill them with goodies you've wrapped in newspaper. Complete the fun with sprigs of greenery and **No-Melt Snowballs**.

Instructions for Snow News begin on page 128.

$\mathcal{S}$et the scene for a whimsical winter wonderland by building a papier-mâché Snow Fellow to stand beside a snow-white **Paper Tree Arrangement**. Use rubber stamps to decorate a Papier-Mâché Platter with playful temperature terms. Fill a **Footed Bowl** with No-Melt Snowballs, and paint red and green spots on a smaller **Dotted Bowl** to add a punch of Christmas color.

A BEACH HOUSE *Christmas*

Whether you live by the sea or just wish you had oceanfront property, this coastal design will make your dreams of a white Christmas come true … beach style! An emphasis on clean lines, refreshing colors, and the use of natural elements produces the look and feel of a seaside holiday getaway.

Instructions for A Beach House Christmas *begin on page 133.*

Make multiples of our Wrapped Candle Holder to set your home and heart aglow.

Create your own collection of custom-made Shell Candles using a variety of pretty seashells. You can use shells you've picked up along the shore or you can purchase them from the craft store. Made using a sand-colored yarn, a Knit Throw lends just the right amount of warmth to the space when combined with a Knit Pillow and an Embellished Pillow.

Bring the outdoors in by filling a large glass compote with sand, rocks, seashells, greenery, and netting ribbon. The Glass Centerpiece will look beautiful gracing a coffee table or a dining table. Resembling a sandy beach, this Table Runner is prime real estate for decorating with a myriad of ocean-inspired accents.

Instructions for A Beach House Christmas begin on page 133.

Liven up a window with a Seaside Swag. The swag is adorned with various seaside treasures and a large cork star.
Fill your tree with glad tidings by stamping plain wooden tags with seasonal sentiments.
A host of embellishments tie these Tag Ornaments to the beach theme.

Play up the nautical theme by embellishing your packages with netting ribbon, seashells, sand dollars, and starfish. Shell-trimmed labels dress up Baskets of Gifts (opposite) that are filled with Gift Boxes and paper sack Gift Bags.

Instructions for A Beach House Christmas begin on page 133.

A unique holiday decoration, Wind Chimes made from seashells and jingle bells sound as pretty as they look! Tuck bleached Starfish Ornaments among the tree branches for a striking touch. Message in a Bottle Ornaments are a fun way to extend season's greetings, and netting ribbon topped with an assortment of ocean wonders creates a beautiful Shell Garland to wind around your tree.

there's no place like

HOME

for the holidays

dd interest to a doorway by hanging a distinctive Cascade instead of the traditional wreath. Suspended by netting ribbon, the flowing design is accentuated with cork stars, jingle bells, and a bleached starfish. Nothing rings in the season quite like jingle bells! A crackle finish gives these Painted Jingle Bells a weathered look that fits in nicely with the oceanfront motif.

Instructions for A Beach House Christmas *begin on page 133.*

Count down the days until Christmas with this eye-catching **Tag Advent Calendar**. As you turn over each day's tag, you'll reveal a jolly message that's sure to boost everyone's holiday spirit.

Instructions for A Beach House Christmas *begin on page 133.*

Send messages of goodwill by placing a **Message in a Bottle** on a table as though it washed up on the shore. Transform a simple basket into a sensational **Serving Tray** that's ideal for serving up holiday fare.

Whimsical Christmas

You're sure to have a cool Yule when this lively St. Nick comes to town! Bursting with flair and whimsy, this lighthearted collection of Christmas decorations will help you create a holly-jolly holiday home.

Instructions for Whimsical Christmas begin on page 137.

Make your mantel merry by dressing it with zany **Painted Christmas Trees** and an assortment of fun and funky **Mantel Packages**.

Christmas will be a ho-ho-whole lot of fun with this North Pole pal! Bearing armloads of presents, the **Whimsical Santa** features candy cane-striped legs and green jingle bell-tipped elf boots. Place the free-standing figure near the fireplace, by the tree, or anywhere you want to add extra cheer.

Instructions for Whimsical Christmas begin on page 137.

Carry out a holiday tradition in style this year by hanging a **Skinny Dotted Knit Stocking** and a Skinny Striped Knit Stocking by the chimney. A patchwork of fun, colorful patterns—stripes, swirls, and spots—this **Painted Tree Skirt** is almost too cute to cover with gifts.

Jazz up your evergreen with this spirited selection of trims—**Ornaments with Knit Collars**, **Dotted Snowy Ornaments**, **Painted Canvas Ornaments**, and a **Star Tree Topper**. This eclectic collection will bring your tree to life, especially when you add a playful **Bottle Cap Garland**.

Instructions for Whimsical Christmas begin on page 137.

Capturing the childlike spirit of Christmas, this stack of **Standing Packages** is a creative way to set the scene for festive gatherings. The bold, colorful designs of the "wrapped" presents tie in nicely with the tree skirt.

icy splendor

Transform your home into an icy palace this Christmas! By fashioning ornaments and accents in shades of wintry white, you'll create a holiday décor that's filled with snowy splendor.

Instructions for Icy Splendor begin on page 143.

Craft a host of **Framed Angel Pictures** to display on your mantel. The delicate images convey all the joy and wonder of the season.

These **Snowflake Stockings** will look magical hanging by the fireplace. The satin-trimmed velvet stockings showcase embossed, beaded, and stamped snowflake motifs. Using velvet in an icy combination of colors (we used white, grey, and cream) adds an element of interest.

Instructions for Icy Splendor *begin on page 143.*

A light dusting of beaded flurries highlights this striking Snowflake Tree Skirt to create an elegant foundation for a wintry-white tree. Fashioned from white, grey, and cream velvet to coordinate with the stockings, the skirt looks splendid with Icy Wrapped Packages.

Instructions for Icy Splendor begin on page 143.

Your holiday tree will be a masterpiece when you decorate it with Silver Leaf Frames. The artful trims are made by applying silver leaf to inexpensive black frames. Use smaller silver leaf frames to create Framed Angel Ornaments. The angel and star motifs are emphasized with glitter and mica flakes for a sparkly finish. A blizzard of Icy Wrapped Packages shimmer with a variety of embellishments. Complete the look by tying glistening ribbons on each gift.

A Bead Garland, crafted from a selection of clear, silver, and smoky beads, will add splendor to your tree. Embossed Leaf Ornaments, Etched Ornaments, and Embossed Snowflake Ornaments extend the wintry theme to every branch. Blanketed by a snowy-white Embossed Velvet Table Runner (*opposite*), a sideboard is the ideal place to showcase a collection of frosty decorations. Illuminate the display with Etched Candle Holders that feature delicate etched snowflakes.

Instructions for Icy Splendor begin on page 143.

Glitter & Glitz

$\mathcal{S}$end out the Invitations right away, because this New Year's party is one your friends won't want to miss! These colorful decorations and scrumptious hors d'oeuvres will help you ring in the year with style. Sequin-trimmed satin Table Banners welcome guests to a night filled with glitter and glitz.

Instructions and recipes for Glitter & Glitz begin on page 145.

A tree trimmed with these dazzling decorations is one you'll want to keep up well into the New Year. The sparkling effect produced by the Glittered Star Topper is repeated by using smaller Glittered Star Ornaments throughout the tree. A neat alternative to traditional trims, Party Hats are a clever way to set the tone for a fun get-together.

$\mathcal{M}$ ade by attaching glittery foam-core numbers onto lengths of wire-edged ribbon, these New Year Ornaments will add a timely touch to your tree. Spinning Ornaments lend dimension and whimsy. Transform ordinary glass ornaments into Glittered and Flocked Balls. This fun-and-easy project will produce one-of-a-kind baubles that will be admired by all.

Instructions and recipes for Glitter & Glitz begin on page 145.

If you want to make a big decorative impact with a not-so-big budget, we have the ideal solution—Hanging Stars and Large Revolving Ornaments. Suspended from the ceiling, the sizable designs can be used randomly throughout the room to add splashes of color. Or consider arranging them to define particular spaces, such as a buffet table or the dance floor. Craft a Sparkly Centerpiece to remind your friends that the future is bright!

Instructions and recipes for Glitter & Glitz begin on page 145.

Lime green **Napkins** embellished with turquoise, orange, and purple ribbons are a playful addition to the table. For a coordinated look, accent a set of **Chargers** with foil origami paper in the same colors. And **Champagne Flute Charms** are a quick and festive way to avoid beverage mix-ups.

*N*ew Year's Eve just wouldn't be the same without Party Horns. Simply embellish purchased party horns to craft this trio of noisemakers—Roll-out Horns, Fringed Horns, and Paper Tube Horns. Glimmering Party Crackers filled with confetti are another celebration must-have. Produce a mood-setting glow with a collection of Striped Candles (opposite).

*C*elebrate auld lang syne by giving your pals Photo CD Party Favors—a compact disc filled with photos you've taken with your friends during the past year. A flashy fabric sleeve makes a fashionable protector.

Instructions and recipes for Glitter & Glitz begin on page 145.

THE SHARING

OF CHRISTMAS

Perhaps you can't recall the very first gift you bestowed upon someone. But in all likelihood, the same warmth of sharing you experienced then still lifts your spirit each Christmas season. And isn't it amazing how that warmth expands into joy when you share gifts made with your own two hands? From amazing accessories to tasty treats, these treasures are your opportunity to create delight within the hearts of everyone you know.

UNDER the TREE

One of the best things about Christmas is gift-giving. It's so exciting to place your gifts under the tree and anticipate the recipients' reactions. Our lineup of handcrafted gifts is sure to result in favorable responses. A present to be treasured, this cheery **Holiday Box** will serve as two gifts in one when you fill it with recipe cards, photos, or other goodies.

Instructions for Under the Tree begin on page 153.

"Snow-body" can resist the charm of this adorable Snow Dude! With dangling arms and legs, he's poised for fun. Using just a little felt and a couple of snowflake buttons, you can transform a pair of purchased house shoes into sprightly Snowman Slippers.

A personalized
Knit Stocking is a
great Christmas gift
idea! Fashioned in
the colors of the
season, the stocking
is embellished with
wooden beads and
tin alphabet stars
that spell out the
recipient's name.

What woman wouldn't love jewelry for Christmas? This uniquely handcrafted Beaded Necklace & Earrings set is an eye-catching ensemble that will add flair to her wardrobe.

They say that a dog is a man's best friend, and this canine is no exception! Crafted from a pair of thick hunting socks and filled with rice, our microwavable Hot Dog Neck Warmer is sure to inspire a case of puppy love.

Instructions for Under the Tree begin on page 153.

Golden North Pole
Nuggets

Golden North Pole Nuggets

1 Package (10 oz) peanut butter morsels
3 tbsp shortening
1 1/2 cups thin pretzel sticks
1 package (6 oz) plain fish shaped crackers

Combine peanut butter morsels and shortening in a
large glass bowl; microwave at HIGH 2 to 2 1/2
minutes, stirring once. Stir in pretzel sticks and
crackers.
Drop mixture by tablespoonfuls onto wax paper.
Let stand 30 minutes or until firm. Store in an
airtight container.
Yield: 2 dozen nuggets

HONEY
BARBECUE
SAUCE

happy holid

To:
The
Harsons

FROM:
the
Kees

Have A Cool Yule!

text
me
season

gifts FOR EVERY taste

Joyful holidays begin with gifts for every taste. From spicy selections to sweet delights, this collection of palate-pleasing presents will have recipients savoring the season. And several of these yummy recipes are easy enough for youngsters to create. Deliver the offerings in handcrafted containers to make your gift even more thoughtful.

Instructions for Gifts for Every Taste *begin on page 156.*

$\mathcal{P}$resented on Candy Clipboards, gifts of **Golden North Pole Nuggets** and Peppermint Candy Cups will have recipients taking note! Kids will love helping whip together the tasty treats, which make great teacher appreciation gifts.

GOLDEN NORTH POLE NUGGETS

    1   package (10 ounces) peanut butter morsels
    2   tablespoons shortening
1 1/2   cups thin pretzel sticks
    1   package (6 ounces) plain fish-shaped crackers

Combine peanut butter morsels and shortening in a large glass bowl; microwave at HIGH 2 to 2 1/2 minutes, stirring once. Stir in pretzel sticks and crackers.

Drop mixture by tablespoonfuls onto wax paper. Let stand 30 minutes or until firm. Store in an airtight container.
Yield: 2 dozen nuggets

PEPPERMINT CANDY CUPS

Peppermint Candy Cups are fun and safe to make because the vanilla-flavored candy coating melts in the microwave oven, not on the stove.

    12   ounces vanilla-flavored candy coating
    3/4   cup crushed hard peppermint candy

Place candy coating in a 2-quart glass bowl; microwave at MEDIUM (50% power) 3 to 4 minutes or until melted, stirring after 2 minutes. Stir in candy. Spoon mixture evenly into petit four paper cups, filling three-fourths full. Chill until firm. Store in an airtight container.
Yield: 3 dozen candies

JUMBO CHOCOLATE CHIP COOKIES

- ½ cup butter or margarine, softened
- ½ cup shortening
- 1 cup firmly packed brown sugar
- ½ cup granulated sugar
- 2 large eggs
- 2 teaspoons vanilla extract
- 2½ cups all-purpose flour
- 1 teaspoon baking soda
- ½ teaspoon salt
- 1 package (12 ounces) semisweet chocolate morsels
- 1 cup chopped pecans

Beat butter and shortening at medium speed with an electric mixer until soft and creamy. Gradually add sugars, beating well. Add eggs and vanilla; beat well. Combine flour, baking soda, and salt; gradually add to butter mixture, beating well. Stir in chocolate morsels and pecans.

Drop dough by scant one-fourth cupfuls onto ungreased baking sheets; flatten each cookie into a 3½-inch circle, making sure the flattened cookies are 2 inches apart. Bake at 350° for 12 minutes. Cool slightly on baking sheets; remove to wire racks and let cool completely.
Yield: 2 dozen cookies

MOCHA LATTE SYRUP
This intensely-flavored syrup will transform hot milk into a coffee lover's delight.

- ¾ cup sugar
- ⅓ cup unsweetened cocoa
- ¼ cup instant espresso
- ½ teaspoon ground cinnamon
- ½ cup water
- 2 tablespoons vanilla extract

Combine sugar, cocoa, espresso, and cinnamon in a medium saucepan. Whisk in water and bring to a boil over medium heat. Boil 1 minute, stirring often. Remove from heat; stir in vanilla. Store in refrigerator up to 2 weeks. Give with serving instructions for Mocha Latte.
Yield: 1¼ cups syrup

MOCHA LATTE
- 1 tablespoon Mocha Latte Syrup
- ¾ cup hot milk

Spoon syrup into a coffee cup; stir in milk.
Yield: 1 serving

Give cool Yule greetings by presenting **Jumbo Chocolate Chip Cookies** in quick-to-make gift bags. The recipe yields two dozen cookies, so you'll have plenty to go around. Your favorite coffee-lover will appreciate a container of **Mocha Latte Syrup**. Decorated with a handmade clay magnet, it's two gifts in one!

Instructions for Gifts for Every Taste begin on page 156.

CHRISTMAS CUPCAKES

Turn your little artists loose on these cupcakes and they'll turn each one into a masterpiece. Provide a full palette of decorator candies to spark their creativity. Candy-coated chocolate candies, licorice, and red cinnamon candies are just a few of the possibilities.

- 1 package (16 ounces) pound cake mix
- ³/₄ cup milk
- 2 large eggs
- ¹/₂ teaspoon vanilla extract
- 1 container (16 ounces) ready-to-spread vanilla frosting
  Assorted candies

Combine the first 4 ingredients in a large mixing bowl; beat at medium speed with an electric mixer 4 minutes.

Line muffin pans with aluminum foil baking cups; fill cups three-fourths full. Bake at 350° for 16 to 18 minutes or until a wooden pick inserted in center comes out clean. Remove from pans and cool on wire racks.

Spread tops of cupcakes with frosting and decorate with candies.

Yield: 16 cupcakes

Note: To make chocolate cupcakes, add ³/₄ cup chocolate syrup to batter. This will make 21 cupcakes.

Children will have a wonderful time decorating Christmas Cupcakes. And you'll want to keep **Little Cherry Pound Cakes** on hand for last-minute gifts.

LITTLE CHERRY POUND CAKES

- 1 jar (10 ounces) maraschino cherries
- ³/₄ cup butter, softened
- ³/₄ cup shortening
- 3 cups sugar
- 6 large eggs
- 3¹/₄ cups all-purpose flour
- ¹/₈ teaspoon salt
- 1 cup milk
- 1 teaspoon almond extract
- 1 teaspoon vanilla extract
  Cherry Glaze (recipe follows)
  Garnish: maraschino cherry halves

Drain jar of cherries, discarding juice. Chop cherries and set aside, reserving ¹/₄ cup for Cherry Glaze.

Beat butter and shortening at medium speed with an electric mixer until creamy. Gradually add sugar, beating 1 minute. Add eggs, 1 at a time, beating just until yellow disappears.

Combine flour and salt; gradually add to butter mixture alternately with milk, beginning and ending with flour mixture. Beat at low speed just until blended. Stir in flavorings and ¹/₂ cup chopped cherries.

Spoon batter into 7 greased and floured 5³/₄ x 3-inch mini foil loafpans. (We recommend greasing your pans with shortening for best results.)

Bake at 300° for 55 minutes or until a wooden pick inserted in center comes out almost clean. Cool in pans on wire racks 10 minutes.

Drizzle Cherry Glaze over slightly warm cakes. Garnish, if desired.

Refrigerate cakes to let glaze harden before wrapping. Wrap cakes individually in cellophane for gift giving.

Yield: 7 mini pound cakes

CHERRY GLAZE

- ¹/₄ cup butter, softened
- 1 package (3 ounces) cream cheese, softened
- 2 cups powdered sugar
- 3 tablespoons milk
- 1 teaspoon vanilla extract
- ¹/₄ cup chopped maraschino cherries (from Little Cherry Pound Cakes recipe)

Beat butter and cream cheese at medium speed with an electric mixer until creamy. Gradually add powdered sugar and milk; beat until smooth. Stir in vanilla and cherries.
Yield: about 2 cups glaze

HONEY BARBECUE SAUCE

- ¹/₄ cup butter or margarine
- 1 medium onion, diced (about 1 cup)
- 1 cup ketchup
- ¹/₃ cup water
- ¹/₄ cup honey
- 2 tablespoons lemon juice
- 1 tablespoon Worcestershire sauce
- ¹/₄ teaspoon ground black pepper

Melt butter in small saucepan over medium heat; add onion and sauté 4 to 5 minutes or until tender. Stir in ketchup and remaining ingredients; bring to a boil. Reduce heat and simmer, uncovered, 5 minutes. Store sauce in refrigerator up to 1 week.
Yield: about 2 cups sauce
Note: You can multiply the recipe for Honey Barbecue Sauce as desired.

A flavorful addition to a variety of meats, homemade Honey Barbecue Sauce is a gift that will be enjoyed by all. A four-nut combination—almonds, pecans, peanuts, and Brazil nuts—is spiced up with a fiery blend of jalapeño pepper sauce and hot sauce to create Jalapeño Nuts. Accent the can with glittery peppers crafted from cardstock.

Instructions for Gifts for Every Taste *begin on page 156.*

JALAPEÑO NUTS

- 1 cup whole almonds
- 1 cup pecan halves
- 1 cup dry-roasted peanuts
- 1 cup Brazil nuts
- ¹/₄ cup butter or margarine
- ¹/₃ cup jalapeño pepper sauce
- 1 tablespoon hot sauce
- 1 tablespoon Worcestershire sauce
- 1¹/₂ teaspoons garlic powder
- 1¹/₂ teaspoons salt
- 1 teaspoon dry mustard

Combine first 4 ingredients in a 15¹/₂ x 10¹/₂-inch jellyroll pan. Bake at 325° for 10 minutes.

Combine butter and remaining ingredients in a saucepan; cook over medium heat, stirring constantly, until butter melts.

Pour over nuts, stirring to coat. Bake an additional 20 minutes, stirring once. Spread nuts on paper towels to cool completely. Store in an airtight container.
Yield: 4 cups nuts

CRAZY MIXED-UP POPCORN

- 6 cups popped popcorn
- 3 cups crisp rice cereal squares
- 2 cups toasted oat O-shaped cereal
- 1 1/2 cups dry roasted peanuts
- 1 cup pecan pieces
- 1 cup firmly packed brown sugar
- 1/2 cup butter or margarine
- 1/4 cup light corn syrup
- 1 teaspoon vanilla extract
- 1/4 teaspoon baking soda

Stir together first 5 ingredients in a lightly greased roasting pan.

Bring brown sugar, butter, and corn syrup to a boil in a 3-quart saucepan over medium heat, stirring constantly. Boil sugar mixture, without stirring, 5 minutes or until a candy thermometer registers 250°. Remove from heat; stir in vanilla and baking soda.

Pour over popcorn mixture and stir until coated.

Bake at 250° for 1 hour, stirring every 20 minutes. Cool in pan on a wire rack; break apart. Store in an airtight container. **Yield:** 14 cups popcorn

TEX-MEX SEASONING

- 3 tablespoons chili powder
- 2 tablespoons ground cumin
- 1 tablespoon ground black pepper
- 1 tablespoon salt
- 1 tablespoon garlic powder
- 1 1/2 teaspoons ground red pepper

Stir together all ingredients and store in an airtight container up to 6 months. Sprinkle on chicken, beef, potatoes, corn, and popped popcorn.
Yield: 1/2 cup seasoning
Note: You can multiply the recipe for Tex-Mex Seasoning as desired.

A pail of **Crazy Mixed-up Popcorn** is sure to please. And a packet of **Tex-Mex Seasoning** will spice up the holidays. Have the kids make fingerprint trees to decorate colorful gift bags.

QUICK BAKING MIX

    10 cups all-purpose flour
    1/3 cup baking powder
    1/4 cup sugar
    1 1/2 tablespoons salt
    2 cups shortening

Combine first 4 ingredients in a large bowl; stir with a wire whisk.

Cut shortening into dry ingredients with a pastry blender until mixture is crumbly. Store in an airtight container at room temperature up to 6 weeks. Give mix with the following recipes.
Yield: 13 cups mix

QUICK-MIX BISCUITS

    2 cups Quick Baking Mix
    1/2 cup milk

Combine Quick Baking Mix and milk, stirring with a fork just until dry ingredients are moistened. Turn dough out onto a heavily floured surface; knead lightly 3 or 4 times.

Roll or pat dough to 1/2-inch thickness; cut out biscuits with a floured 2-inch biscuit cutter. Place biscuits on an ungreased baking sheet; bake at 450° for 10 minutes or until lightly browned.
Yield: 10 biscuits

QUICK-MIX BANANA-NUT MUFFINS

    1 package (8 ounces) cream cheese, softened
    1 cup sugar
    2 large eggs
    1 cup mashed ripe banana
    1/2 teaspoon vanilla extract
    2 cups Quick Baking Mix
    1/2 cup chopped pecans

Beat cream cheese at high speed with an electric mixer until creamy; gradually add sugar, beating well. Add eggs; beat well. Add banana and vanilla; beat well. Stir in Quick Baking Mix and pecans.

Spoon batter into lightly greased muffin pans, filling two-thirds full. Bake at 375° for 20 to 22 minutes or until golden. Remove from pans immediately.
Yield: 20 muffins

QUICK-MIX PANCAKES

    3 cups Quick Baking Mix
    1 1/2 cups milk
    2 large eggs, lightly beaten

Combine all ingredients; beat with a wire whisk until smooth.

For each pancake, pour about 1/4 cup batter onto a hot, lightly greased griddle. Cook pancakes until tops are covered with bubbles and edges look cooked; turn and cook other sides.
Yield: 16 pancakes

Send caring thoughts with a gift for the family to enjoy together—Quick Baking Mix. Give them their choice of Christmas morning delights by including recipes for biscuits, banana-nut muffins, and pancakes. A sweet snowman card and the recipe cards are attached to the container with jumbo rickrack.

Instructions for Gifts for Every Taste begin on page 156.

THE TASTES

OF CHRISTMAS

It isn't Christmas until everyone partakes of table-groaning feasts, nibbles on seasonal treats, and shares desserts that are destined to star in holiday reminiscences for years to come. Whether you're hosting Christmas for the first or the fifty-first time, you'll want to add plenty of these scrumptious recipes to your list of new family favorites.

Dinner at the Mansion

Create for your honored guests a holiday feast enjoyed by visitors to the Arkansas Governor's Mansion. Decked out in Christmas finery, the Georgian colonial-style home welcomes guests with Southern hospitality.

$\mathcal{D}$ecorated with violins, a tree themed "The Symphony of Christmas" fills the entryway with classic charm. A **Chocolate Sugarplum Cheese Ball** is a delightfully different appetizer.

CHOCOLATE SUGARPLUM CHEESE BALL

- 2 packages (8 ounces each) cream cheese, softened
- ¼ cup butter softened
- 1½ cups sugar
- ⅓ cup cocoa
- 2 tablespoons light corn syrup
- ½ cup finely chopped dried figs
- ½ cup golden raisins
- ½ cup finely chopped dried apricots
- 2 tablespoons almond extract
- 1 package (8 ounces) pecans, finely chopped
  Garnish: chopped dried apricots
  Gingersnaps and/or chocolate graham crackers to serve

Beat cream cheese, butter, sugar, cocoa, and corn syrup with an electric mixer until creamy and smooth. Add figs, raisins, apricots, and almond extract; mix thoroughly. Shape into a ball and coat with finely chopped pecans. Garnish, if desired. Serve with gingersnaps and/or chocolate graham crackers.

Yield: one 7-inch cheese ball

APPLE AND SQUASH SOUP

- 1 pound butternut squash, peeled, seeded, and cut into pieces
- 3 Granny Smith apples, peeled, cored, and cut into pieces
- 1 medium onion, chopped
- ¼ teaspoon rosemary
- ¼ teaspoon marjoram
- 3 cans (10¾ ounces each) chicken broth
- 4 cups water
- 2 slices white bread
  Salt and pepper to taste
- ½ cup whipping cream
  Garnish: whipping cream

Combine squash, apples, onion, rosemary, marjoram, chicken broth, water, and bread in a large saucepan; salt and pepper to taste. Bring mixture to a boil and simmer, uncovered, 45 minutes; cool.

Place half of mixture at a time in a blender and purée. Return to saucepan and bring to a boil. Remove from heat and stir in cream. Garnish, if desired. Serve hot.

Soup can be made ahead and refrigerated after it is puréed. Add cream when ready to serve.

Yield: 10 cups soup

HEARTS OF ROMAINE WITH CRANBERRY VINAIGRETTE

- ½ cup whole berry cranberry sauce
- 2 tablespoons balsamic vinegar
- ½ teaspoon grated orange zest
- 2 tablespoons fresh orange juice
- 1½ teaspoons Dijon mustard
- ½ teaspoon honey
- ⅛ teaspoon salt
- ¼ cup olive oil
  Hearts of romaine lettuce
  Garnish: toasted sliced almonds and dried cranberries

Stir cranberry sauce, vinegar, orange zest, orange juice, mustard, honey, and salt until well blended in a bowl. Stir in olive oil, 1 tablespoon at a time, until well blended. Pour dressing over lettuce. Garnish, if desired.

Yield: 1 cup vinaigrette

Creamy Apple and Squash Soup (*above*), accompanied by **Hearts of Romaine with Cranberry Vinaigrette**, is a delicious start to any meal. For a simple garnish, an apple peel is coiled into an elegant rosette. Stately menu cards (*right*) are prominently placed to heighten anticipation for each course.

$\mathcal{G}$uests will savor this sumptuous fare—**Parmesan Encrusted Salmon Fillets** topped with **Key Lime Beurre Blanc**, **Rice and Fruit Dressing**, and **Green Beans with Almonds**. The Lenox china features 25 gold diamonds on the outer rim to denote that Arkansas was the 25th state admitted into the Union and is the only state with a working diamond mine.

PARMESAN ENCRUSTED SALMON FILLETS

- $^{1}/_{2}$ cup all-purpose flour
- $^{1}/_{2}$ cup grated Parmesan cheese
- 1 teaspoon salt
- $^{1}/_{4}$ teaspoon pepper
- 4 salmon fillets (4 to 6 ounces each)
- 2 tablespoons olive oil
  Key Lime Beurre Blanc (recipe follows)

Combine flour, cheese, salt, and pepper. Cover salmon with cheese mixture until well coated. Sauté salmon in olive oil over medium heat until golden brown on both sides.

Serve with Key Lime Beurre Blanc.

Yield: 4 servings

KEY LIME BEURRE BLANC

- 2 cups white wine
- 1 whole onion, cut julienne style
- 1 tablespoon whipping cream
- 1 cup cold butter, cut into pieces
  Juice of 1 lemon
- 3 tablespoons key lime juice

Cook wine and onion in a saucepan over medium heat until wine is reduced to 3 to 4 tablespoons. Add cream and cook 1 minute. Whisk in butter until melted. Stir in lemon and key lime juice. Serve sauce over salmon.

If making sauce ahead, do not refrigerate or reheat. Keep at room temperature.

Yield: 2$^{1}/_{4}$ cups sauce

RICE AND FRUIT DRESSING

    4 cups chicken broth
  1/2 cup butter or margarine
  1/4 cup lemon juice
    2 cups uncooked brown rice
  1/2 cup raisins
  1/2 cup chopped dried apricots
  1/2 cup chopped onion

Bring chicken broth, butter, and lemon juice to a boil. Stir in rice, raisins, apricots, and onion. Reduce heat to medium-low, cover, and cook 1 hour or until rice is tender.
Yield: 8 to 10 servings

GREEN BEANS WITH ALMONDS

    8 ounces bacon, diced
    6 ounces slivered almonds
    2 bags (14 ounces each) frozen whole green beans
    1 red bell pepper, cut into strips
    2 teaspoons garlic powder or granulated garlic
    2 teaspoons salt
  1/2 teaspoon black pepper

Sauté bacon and almonds in skillet over medium heat until bacon is crisp, being careful not to burn almonds. Add green beans and bell pepper. Season with garlic, salt, and black pepper. Cook until green beans are tender.
Yield: 8 servings

*Wrapped in a crisp white linen napkin to retain their warmth, **Fennel and Coarse Salt Breadsticks** are irresistible.*

FENNEL AND COARSE SALT BREADSTICKS

    1 package active dry yeast (2 1/2 teaspoons)
1 1/2 teaspoons sugar, divided
  3/4 cup warm water
2 1/2 cups all-purpose flour, divided
    1 teaspoon salt
  1/4 cup olive oil
  1/3 cup yellow cornmeal
    1 egg white
    1 tablespoon water
    2 tablespoons fennel seeds
    2 tablespoons coarse salt

In a large bowl of an electric mixer, proof yeast with 1/2 teaspoon of sugar in 3/4 cup warm water for 5 minutes or until it is foamy. Add remaining 1 teaspoon sugar, 2 cups flour, salt, and oil; beat mixture with the dough hook until it is well combined. Knead dough, kneading in enough of remaining 1/2 cup flour to make the dough form a ball. Knead dough for 5 minutes or until it is soft but not sticky.

On a lightly floured surface, cover dough and let rest for 15 minutes. Divide the dough into 12 pieces. Working with 1 piece at a time and keeping the remaining pieces covered, roll dough between palms of hands to form a 14-inch-long rope. Place ropes 2 inches apart on baking sheets sprinkled lightly with cornmeal.

Cover and let rise in a warm place (80° to 85°) for 40 minutes. Mix egg white and 1 tablespoon water in a small bowl. Brush dough lightly with egg wash and sprinkle with fennel seeds and coarse salt.

Bake on center rack in a preheated 450° oven for 12 to 15 minutes or until lightly browned. Let cool on a wire rack for 10 minutes. Breadsticks may be made 1 day in advance and kept in an airtight container.
Yield: 12 breadsticks

RASPBERRY-ORANGE BAVARIAN CREAM

2½ pints fresh or 5 cups frozen raspberries
6 tablespoons Grand Marnier, divided
½ cup plus 2 tablespoons orange juice
3 tablespoons plain gelatin
½ cup plus 2 tablespoons cold water
¾ cup honey
5 teaspoons grated orange zest
2½ cups whipping cream
1¾ cups plus 2 tablespoons sour cream
Garnish: whipped cream and fresh raspberries

Purée raspberries in a food processor; strain. Discard seeds. Stir in 5 tablespoons Grand Marnier. Divide into 2 bowls with one bowl having ¾ of the mixture and the other bowl having ¼ of the mixture.

In a separate bowl, stir in remaining 1 tablespoon Grand Marnier into orange juice.

In a small saucepan, sprinkle gelatin over cold water and let stand for 3 to 5 minutes to soften. Stir in honey and orange zest. Heat until mixture simmers. Remove from heat. Stir in whipping cream and sour cream.

Stir half the cream mixture into bowl containing the larger portion of raspberry mixture. Stir orange juice mixture into the remaining cream mixture.

Spoon 2 tablespoons berry/cream mixture into 1-cup serving glasses. Chill until set.

Divide orange juice/cream mixture evenly in glasses. Chill until set.

Top each dessert with remaining berry mixture. Chill overnight. Garnish, if desired.
Yield: about 8 servings

CHOCOLATE AND PEANUT GELATO PIE
Crust
1½ cups sugar-free chocolate cookie crumbs
¾ cup peanuts, ground
2 tablespoons sugar substitiute
3 tablespoons butter, melted

Combine cookie crumbs, peanuts, and sugar substitute. Add melted butter and stir. Press mixture into a 9-inch pie plate. Bake at 350° for 10 minutes; cool.

Filling
½ gallon fat-free vanilla ice cream, softened
1 cup peanuts

Combine ice cream with peanuts; pour into crust. Freeze overnight.

Fudge Sauce
1 cup sugar substitute
1 cup light corn syrup
½ cup cocoa
4 tablespoons butter
¼ cup half and half
½ teaspoon vanilla extract
⅛ teaspoon salt

Combine sugar substitute, corn syrup, cocoa, butter, and half and half in a saucepan. Bring to a boil. Boil 3 minutes, stirring constantly. Remove from heat; add vanilla and salt. Cool and drizzle over pie.
Yield: one 9-inch pie

Under the direction of Don Bingham, Mansion Administrator, chefs Jason Knapp and Clark Huff enjoy preparing such delightful delicacies as **Raspberry-Orange Bavarian Cream.** One of Governor Mike Huckabee's favorites, this low-sugar **Chocolate and Peanut Gelato Pie** is packed with flavor.

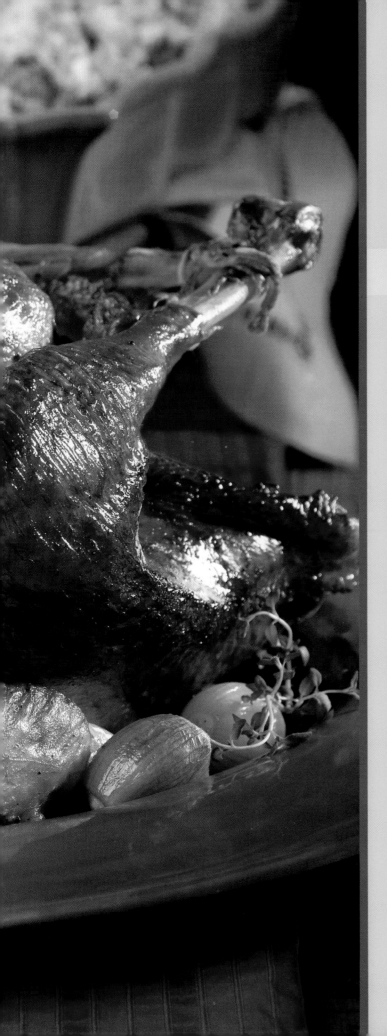

CHRISTMAS
cookery 101

You're not alone—even the best of cooks had to prepare that "first Christmas dinner." And we're here to ensure that your Yuletide debut is a huge success! We've gone back to the basics to help you cook a delectably moist Roast Turkey with Thyme Butter and Shallots, Old-Fashioned Cornbread Dressing, and Last-Minute Gravy that even your grandmother would be proud to serve. So let's get cooking!

OLD-FASHIONED CORNBREAD DRESSING

Understanding cooking terms makes cooking much more fun and successful. In this recipe we explain how to sauté vegetables.

- 2 cups cornmeal
- 2 teaspoons baking powder
- 1 teaspoon baking soda
- 1/2 teaspoon salt
- 2 cups buttermilk
- 2 large eggs, beaten
- 2 tablespoons bacon drippings, melted
- 3 stalks celery, chopped
- 1 medium onion, chopped
- 1/3 cup butter or margarine
- 12 slices day-old bread, crumbled
- 1 can (10 3/4 ounces) chicken broth
- 1 cup water
- 1 cup milk
- 2 large eggs, beaten
- 1 teaspoon poultry seasoning
- 1 teaspoon rubbed sage
- 1/4 teaspoon salt
- 1/4 teaspoon pepper

1. Combine cornmeal, baking powder, baking soda, and salt in a large bowl; add buttermilk, 2 eggs, and melted bacon drippings, stirring well.

2. Place a well-greased 10-inch cast-iron skillet in a 450° oven for 4 minutes or until hot. Remove skillet from oven; spoon batter into skillet. Bake at 450° for 25 minutes or until cornbread is lightly browned. Cool; crumble cornbread into a large bowl.

3. Sautéing is cooking food in a small amount of hot fat, usually butter or oil. To sauté celery and onion, melt butter in a skillet over medium heat. Add celery and onion, stirring until celery is tender and onion is transparent. Add sautéed vegetables, bread, and remaining ingredients to crumbled cornbread, stirring well.

4. Spoon dressing into a lightly greased 13 x 9-inch pan. Bake at 350° for 25 to 30 minutes.

5. After serving, refrigerate any remaining dressing.

Yield: 8 servings

ROAST TURKEY WITH THYME BUTTER AND SHALLOTS

Everyone needs to know how to cook a turkey. If you're diligent about basting this bird near the end of roasting, you'll end up with moist, golden results. Plump shallots nestled around the turkey are caramelized in the pan drippings as they roast and make an easy decoration for the platter. The shallots and thyme butter add a delicious flavor to the turkey. Find shallots and fresh thyme in the produce section of your local grocery.

- 1 turkey (14 pounds)
  Salt and pepper
- 1 large onion
- 3/4 cup unsalted butter, softened
- 2 tablespoons chopped fresh thyme
- 12 large shallots
- 2 tablespoons olive oil
  Last-Minute Gravy (recipe follows)
  Garnish: fresh thyme sprigs

1. Remove giblets and neck from turkey; set aside for another use. Rinse turkey with cold water; pat dry. Sprinkle cavities with salt and pepper. Place turkey, breast side up, in a greased broiler pan.

2. Place onion in body cavity. Tie legs together with heavy string or tuck them under flap of skin. Lift wingtips up and over back, and tuck under bird (photo 1).

3. Combine butter and 2 tablespoons chopped thyme, stirring well. Using fingers, carefully loosen skin from turkey, working up to breast and neck area (photo 2). Refer to photo 3 to spread 1/4 cup of butter mixture under skin (remaining butter will be used later).

4. Generously rub salt and pepper over turkey. Insert a meat thermometer into meaty part of thigh without touching the bone. Place aluminum foil loosely over turkey to form a tent; roast at 325° for 1 hour.

5. Melt remaining butter mixture in a small saucepan over low heat; set aside for basting.

6. Peel shallots and place in a bowl; drizzle with olive oil and sprinkle generously with salt and pepper. Set aside.

7. Uncover turkey; baste with several tablespoons melted butter mixture. Roast 1 hour, basting occasionally with butter mixture. After second hour of roasting, scatter shallots in pan around turkey; baste turkey. Roast 1 more hour or until thermometer registers 180°, basting turkey and shallots every 15 minutes with butter mixture and pan drippings.

8. When turkey is done, carefully transfer it to a serving platter; arrange shallots around turkey. Cover with foil and let turkey rest 15 minutes before carving. Reserve ¹/₂ cup drippings in pan for Last-Minute Gravy. Prepare gravy. Garnish platter just before serving, if desired.

9. After serving, use carcass to make Cream of Turkey and Rice Soup (page 98) or freeze for a later use, if desired.

Yield: 14 servings
Note: If you buy a frozen turkey, remember to allow at least 3 days for it to thaw in the refrigerator.

1. Lift wingtips up and over back, and tuck under bird.

2. Loosen skin from turkey without detaching or tearing skin.

3. Carefully place the butter mixture under skin; replace skin.

Last-Minute Gravy

Don't clean your broiler pan before making gravy—that's where all the goodness is. We suggest whisking the gravy right in the same pan while the turkey rests on a platter. Begin with a roux made from flour and pan drippings. It will add flavor and thicken the gravy (see Cream of Turkey and Rice Soup recipe on page 98 for more information about a roux).

- ¹/₂ cup reserved pan drippings
- ¹/₂ cup all-purpose flour
- 1¹/₂ cups apple cider
- 1¹/₂ cups chicken broth
- ³/₄ teaspoon salt
- ³/₄ teaspoon pepper

1. Set broiler pan containing reserved pan drippings over 2 burners. Whisk flour into drippings in pan. Cook over medium heat until flour mixture (roux) is dark golden, stirring constantly to loosen any browned bits from bottom of pan.

2. Gradually add cider and broth; cook, stirring constantly, 5 to 10 minutes or until gravy is thickened. Stir in salt and pepper.

Yield: 3 cups gravy

AMBROSIA

The key to a tasty ambrosia is to completely remove the pith from the orange sections. The bitter-tasting pith is the white part of the orange between the peel and the fruit. Learning to section an orange will also give you a prettier salad.

   9 navel oranges
   2 cans (20 ounces each) pineapple chunks, drained
   1 cup honey
   1 cup sweetened flaked coconut
   1 to 2 teaspoons almond extract
     Garnish: stemmed maraschino cherries

1. See photos to prepare oranges.

2. Combine first 5 ingredients in a large bowl and stir gently; cover and chill at least 8 hours.

3. Garnish, if desired.

Yield: 8 servings

1. To section an orange, first peel it with a paring knife and be sure to remove the white pith.

2. Holding fruit over a bowl to catch juices, slice between membrane and one orange segment; then, lift the segment out with the knife blade.

Said to be the food of the gods, Ambrosia is a time-honored, holiday fruit salad. Your guests will never suspect that it was so simple to prepare. Once you learn how to properly peel and section the oranges, you've got it made! Use your pretty stemware for an attractive presentation.

Super Dinner Rolls

What can be better than homemade rolls! They aren't as difficult to make as you might think. Once you learn how to knead and proof the dough, you will get wonderful results. Using a cooking thermometer is important. If the liquid you add to your flour mixture is too hot, it will kill the yeast, and if it is too cold, it will keep the dough from rising.

7¼ cups bread flour, divided
¾ cup sugar
2 packages active dry yeast
1 teaspoon salt
2 cups whole milk
½ cup unsalted butter
3 eggs, lightly beaten
1 tablespoon bread flour

1. Combine 2 cups flour, sugar, yeast, and salt in a large mixing bowl; stir well. Combine milk and butter in a saucepan; heat until butter melts, stirring occasionally. Cool to 120° to 130°. Gradually add milk mixture to flour mixture, beating well at low speed with an electric mixer. Beat an additional 2 minutes at medium speed. Add eggs and ¾ cup flour, beating 2 minutes at medium speed. Gradually stir in enough of the remaining 4½ cups flour to make a soft dough.

2. Sprinkle 1 tablespoon flour evenly over work surface. Turn dough out onto floured surface and knead (photo 1) until smooth and elastic (about 8 to 10 minutes). Place dough in a large well-greased bowl, turning to grease top (photo 2). Referring to photo 3, cover dough and let rise (also called proofing) in a warm place (85°), free from drafts, 45 minutes or until doubled in bulk (photo 4).

3. Punch dough down (photo 5); divide in half. Divide each half into 11 equal portions; shape each portion into a ball. Place at least 1 inch apart on large greased baking sheets. Cover and let rise in a warm place, free from drafts, 30 minutes or until doubled in bulk.

4. Bake at 325° for 18 to 20 minutes or until lightly browned. Remove rolls from baking sheets; let cool on wire racks.

Yield: 22 rolls

1. Use the heel of one or both hands to knead dough by pushing the dough down and away from you. Turn, fold, and push down again. Continue this procedure for the time indicated in the recipe.

2. Place dough in a greased bowl and turn dough over to grease top.

3. The ideal proofing temperature is 85°. (We use an oven with a pan of very hot water under the bowl of dough.)

4. Test the dough by pressing two fingers ½ inch into dough. If fingerprints remain, dough is ready to be shaped.

5. Punch dough down with your fist and fold dough into the center.

CREAM OF TURKEY AND RICE SOUP

This is a delicious soup because you are using the turkey bones to make the stock. It takes a little time, but the rich flavor is worth every minute! You will also learn to make a roux with butter and flour that will thicken the liquid.

    1   turkey carcass
   ½   cup butter or margarine
   ½   cup all-purpose flour
    1   large onion, chopped (about 1½ cups)
    2   shallots, chopped
    3   large carrots, scraped and chopped
    3   stalks celery, sliced
    1   cup uncooked long-grain rice
   1½   teaspoons salt
   ½   teaspoon pepper
    2   teaspoons chopped fresh thyme or ½ teaspoon
        dried thyme
    1   cup whipping cream
        Garnish: fresh thyme sprigs

1. Add flour to butter in pan and cook, stirring constantly. This is the first stage of a roux.

2. Cook and stir roux until it turns a blonde color.

1. Place turkey carcass in a large Dutch oven; add water to cover. Bring to a boil; cover, reduce heat, and simmer 1 hour. Remove carcass from liquid, reserving 10 cups stock. Cool carcass and pick meat from bones. Set meat aside.

2. Melt butter in stockpot over medium-high heat. Add flour and cook 5 minutes, stirring constantly. Make a blonde-colored roux following photos 1 and 2.

3. Add onion, shallots, carrot, and celery to roux; reduce heat to medium. Cook 10 minutes, stirring often.

4. Stir in reserved stock, turkey meat, rice, salt, pepper, and thyme; bring to a boil. Cover, reduce heat, and simmer 20 minutes or until rice is tender.

5. Add whipping cream; simmer, uncovered, 5 minutes or to desired thickness.

6. Garnish, if desired.

Yield: about 4 quarts soup

Making your own turkey stock will give this **Cream of Turkey and Rice Soup** its deliciously rich flavor.

1. Gently crack egg, break shell into two halves, and transfer yolk back and forth until all white has drained.

2. Boil sugar syrup until it reaches hard-ball stage on a candy thermometer.

3. Beat egg whites at high speed with an electric mixer while adding hot syrup in a heavy stream.

4. Once divinity holds its shape upon beating, spoon it out by teaspoonfuls onto wax paper.

CLASSIC DIVINITY

Making divinity can be tricky, but knowing the correct methods for separating eggs, beating egg whites, cooking candy syrup, and adding the syrup to beaten egg whites will make you a pro quickly. A big hint to perfect divinity is to pick a dry, cool day to make it. Humidity and candy-making don't mix well.

- 1 cup chopped pecans, toasted
- 2 egg whites
- 2½ cups sugar
- ½ cup water
- ½ cup light corn syrup
- 1 teaspoon vanilla extract

1. To toast pecans, spread pecans on an ungreased baking sheet. Stirring occasionally, bake in a 350° oven 5 to 8 minutes or until pecans are slightly darker in color.

2. See photo 1 to separate the eggs. Beat egg whites in a large mixing bowl at high speed with an electric mixer until stiff peaks form.

3. Combine sugar, water, and corn syrup in a 3-quart saucepan and cook over low heat, stirring constantly, until sugar dissolves. Cover and cook over medium heat 2 to 3 minutes to wash down sugar crystals from sides of pan.

4. Uncover and attach a candy thermometer to pan (photo 2), making sure thermometer does not touch bottom of pan. Cook, uncovered, over medium heat, without stirring, to hard-ball stage (approximately 250° to 268°). You can also test hard-ball stage by dropping a teaspoonful of syrup into a cup of cold water. Syrup forms a hard, yet pliable ball when removed from the water. Remove pan from heat.

5. Pour hot sugar mixture in a heavy stream over beaten egg whites while beating constantly at high speed as shown in photo 3. Add vanilla and continue beating just until mixture holds its shape (3 to 4 minutes). Stir in pecans.

6. Working quickly, drop divinity by rounded teaspoonfuls onto wax paper (see photo 4); cool. Peel from wax paper.

Yield: 2½ dozen candies

Cherry Divinity: Substitute 1 cup finely chopped red candied cherries for pecans.

Delight family and friends by whipping up a sweet sensation—homemade **Classic Divinity**. Our basic candy-making instructions make it easy. For a tasty variation, use red candied cherries instead of pecans.

Sweet CHRISTMAS Celebration

The holidays are an ideal time for getting together with friends to enjoy good times and good food. Sweeten your Christmas celebration with this selection of delectable desserts and seasonal beverages to give your party a flavorful finale!

Encircled by crushed peppermint candies, this Red Velvet Peppermint Cake is soon to become a Yuletide essential.

RED VELVET PEPPERMINT CAKE

- 1 package (18.25 ounces) white cake mix
- 1⅓ cups buttermilk
- 3 egg whites
- 2 tablespoons vegetable oil
- 1 package (9 ounces) yellow cake mix or 1¾ cups yellow cake mix
- ½ cup buttermilk
- 1 large egg
- 2 tablespoons liquid red food coloring
- 1½ tablespoons cocoa
- 1 teaspoon cider vinegar
- ½ teaspoon baking soda
  Peppermint Cream Cheese Frosting (recipe follows)
  Garnish: crushed hard peppermint candies

Beat first 4 ingredients with an electric mixer according to cake mix package directions.

Beat yellow cake mix and next 6 ingredients according to package directions. Spoon red batter alternately with white batter into 3 greased and floured 9-inch round cake pans. Swirl batter gently with a knife.

Bake at 350° for 18 minutes or until a wooden pick inserted in center comes out clean. Cool in pans on wire racks 10 minutes. Remove from pans; cool on wire racks.

Spread Peppermint Cream Cheese Frosting between layers and on top and sides of cake. (Cake may be chilled up to 2 days or frozen up to 1 month.) Garnish, if desired. Serve within 2 hours.

Yield: one 3-layer cake

Note: If cake is frozen, thaw completely before garnishing to prevent candy from running. Do not refrigerate after garnishing.

PEPPERMINT CREAM CHEESE FROSTING

- 1 package (8 ounces) cream cheese, softened
- 1 cup butter or margarine, softened
- 1 package (2 pounds) powdered sugar
- 2 teaspoons peppermint extract or vanilla extract

Beat cream cheese and butter at medium speed with an electric mixer until creamy. Gradually add sugar, beating at low speed until smooth. Add extract, beating until blended.

Yield: about 5 cups frosting

Note: For a quick peppermint frosting, stir together three 16-ounce containers ready-to-spread cream cheese frosting and 2 teaspoons peppermint extract.

CRANBERRY-STREUSEL BARS

- 1 cup fresh cranberries
- 2 tablespoons granulated sugar
- 2⅓ cups all-purpose flour, divided
- ½ teaspoon baking soda
- 2 cups uncooked regular oats
- ½ cup granulated sugar
- ½ cup firmly packed light brown sugar
- 1 cup butter or margarine, cut in pieces
- 1 package (8 ounces) chopped dates
- 1¼ cups chopped pecans
- ¾ cup butterscotch ice cream topping

Stir together cranberries and 2 tablespoons granulated sugar in a small bowl; set aside.

Combine 2 cups flour and next 5 ingredients in a food processor; pulse just until crumbly. Reserve 1 cup flour mixture. Press remaining mixture into bottom of a lightly greased 13 x 9-inch baking pan.

Bake at 350° for 15 minutes or until lightly browned. Sprinkle with dates, pecans, and cranberry mixture. Stir together butterscotch topping and remaining ⅓ cup flour; spoon over cranberries. Sprinkle with reserved 1 cup flour mixture. Bake 20 more minutes or until lightly browned. Cool on a wire rack. Cut into bars.

Yield: 2 dozen bars

Spread Christmas cheer with Cranberry-Streusel Bars. A mixtur of cranberries, dates, pecans, and butterscotch gives these treats th palate-pleasing appeal.

Chocolate, cream cheese, cookies, and coconut are combined to create this lusciously layered **Black and White Cheesecake**.

BLACK AND WHITE CHEESECAKE

Big chips of coconut spike the soft whipped cream that covers this dark cheesecake.

1½   cups shortbread cookie crumbs
2   tablespoons granulated sugar
3   tablespoons butter or margarine, melted
¾   cup butter or margarine
8   squares (1 ounce each) semisweet baking chocolate
1   package (8 ounces) cream cheese, softened
1   package (3 ounces) cream cheese, softened
½   cup granulated sugar
3   large eggs
⅓   cup cream of coconut
1¼   cups whipping cream
2   tablespoons powdered sugar
½   teaspoon vanilla extract
1   package (3 ounces) coconut chips or flaked coconut

Combine first 3 ingredients; stir well. Press into bottom of a greased 9-inch springform pan. Bake at 350° for 10 to 12 minutes or until toasted. Remove from oven and reduce oven temperature to 300°.

Combine ¾ cup butter and chocolate in a heavy saucepan. Cook over medium-low heat until melted, stirring often. Remove from heat and let cool.

Beat cream cheese at medium speed with an electric mixer until creamy. Add ½ cup granulated sugar; beat well. Add eggs, one at a time, beating just until blended after each addition. Stir in cooled chocolate mixture and cream of coconut. Pour over crust in pan. Bake at 300° for 40 minutes or until cheesecake is barely set. Let cool to room temperature in pan on a wire rack; cover and chill 8 hours.

Beat whipping cream at high speed with an electric mixer until foamy; gradually add powdered sugar, beating until soft peaks form. Add vanilla; beat just until blended.

Carefully remove sides of springform pan. Place cheesecake on serving plate. Frost top and sides with whipped cream mixture. Gently press coconut onto sides and sprinkle on top of frosted cheesecake. Chill thoroughly.
Yield: one 9-inch cheesecake

*P*umpkin Chess Pie is a Southern favorite that will be a winner with dessert lovers everywhere! Topped with succulently sweet **Praline Sauce**, this pie is too good to resist.

PUMPKIN CHESS PIE

½ (15-ounce) package refrigerated piecrusts
1 can (15 ounces) pumpkin
½ cup half-and-half
3 eggs
1½ teaspoons vanilla extract
2 cups sugar
¼ cup butter or margarine, melted
¾ teaspoon salt
½ teaspoon ground cinnamon
¼ teaspoon ground ginger
¼ teaspoon ground cloves
Praline Sauce (recipe follows)

Place piecrust in a 9-inch pie plate; fold edges under and crimp. Beat pumpkin and next 9 ingredients at medium speed with an electric mixer until smooth.

Pour pumpkin mixture into prepared piecrust. Bake at 350° for 1 hour and 15 minutes or until knife inserted in center comes out clean. Cool completely on a wire rack. Serve with Praline Sauce.

Yield: one 9-inch pie

Note: For 12 servings, you will need to make 2 pies, but you will have enough Praline Sauce from just one recipe.

PRALINE SAUCE

This rich sauce is also good spooned over ice cream.

1 cup firmly packed brown sugar
½ cup half-and-half
½ cup butter or margarine
½ cup chopped pecans, toasted
½ teaspoon vanilla extract

Combine first 3 ingredients in a small saucepan over medium heat. Bring to a boil; cook 1 minute, stirring constantly. Remove from heat; stir in pecans and vanilla. Cool slightly; serve warm sauce over slices of Pumpkin Chess Pie.

Yield: 2 cups sauce

RUDOLPH'S COOKIES

Red currant jelly dollops Christmas color on these pecan-coated thumbprint cookies.

1 cup butter, softened
¾ cup sugar
2 large eggs, separated
1 teaspoon almond extract
2 cups all-purpose flour
¼ teaspoon salt
1¼ teaspoons ground cinnamon
1¼ cups finely chopped pecans
Red currant jelly

Beat butter at medium speed with an electric mixer until creamy. Gradually add sugar, beating well. Add egg yolks and almond extract, beating until blended.

Combine flour, salt, and cinnamon. Add flour mixture to butter mixture, blending at low speed. Cover and chill dough 1 hour.

Shape dough into 1-inch balls. Lightly beat egg whites. Dip each ball in egg white; roll in pecans. Place 2 inches apart on ungreased baking sheets. Press thumb in each cookie to make an indentation.

Bake at 350° for 15 minutes. Cool 1 minute on baking sheets; remove to wire racks to cool completely. Press centers again with thumb while cookies are still warm; fill center of each cookie with jelly.

Yield: 40 cookies

Note: Using a 1-inch scoop to measure dough portions before rolling into balls will make more uniform cookies.

CRISPY PECAN STICKS

¾ cup butter, softened
¼ cup powdered sugar
2 cups all-purpose flour
¼ teaspoon salt
1 cup chopped pecans
1 tablespoon vanilla extract
2 tablespoons ice water
Powdered sugar

Beat butter at medium speed with an electric mixer until creamy; gradually add ¼ cup powdered sugar, beating well.

Combine flour and salt; add to butter mixture, beating at low speed with an electric mixer until blended. Stir in pecans, vanilla, and ice water.

Roll dough into 1-inch balls and shape into 3-inch sticks. Place sticks on lightly greased baking sheets.

Bake at 350° for 12 to 15 minutes or until browned. Roll in additional powdered sugar. Store in airtight container 2 weeks or freeze 2 months.

Yield: about 3 dozen cookies

*T*reat your holiday guests to a collection of temptingly rich confections—Rudolph's Cookies, Merry Cherry Fudge, and Crispy Pecan Sticks.

MERRY CHERRY FUDGE

Chocolate-covered cherries have some new competition. This easy fudge recipe plants a sweet cherry in every square.

Cooking spray
36 maraschino cherries with stems
1 package (12 ounces) semisweet chocolate morsels
6 squares (1 ounce each) bittersweet baking chocolate, chopped
1 can (14 ounces) sweetened condensed milk
1 teaspoon maraschino cherry juice
1 cup chopped pecans

Lightly coat an 8-inch square pan with cooking spray. Set aside. Blot cherries dry with paper towels.

Combine chocolates in a microwave-safe bowl; microwave on HIGH 1½ to 2 minutes, stirring every 30 seconds until chocolate is smooth. Stir in sweetened condensed milk and cherry juice. Stir in pecans. Spoon mixture into prepared pan. Immediately press cherries into fudge, leaving top of each cherry and stem exposed. Cover and chill fudge 2 hours or until firm.

Cut fudge into 36 squares. Store in an airtight container in refrigerator.

Yield: 2 pounds fudge

COFFEE-KAHLÚA PUNCH

8¼ cups hot strongly brewed coffee
⅓ cup sugar
4 cups milk
1 tablespoon vanilla extract
1¼ cups Kahlúa or other coffee-
    flavored liqueur
5 cups vanilla ice cream, softened
1 square (1 ounce) semisweet baking
    chocolate, coarsely grated

Combine coffee and sugar, stirring until sugar dissolves. Stir in milk and vanilla; cover and chill. Combine chilled coffee mixture and Kahlúa in a punch bowl; stir well. Add ice cream, a few tablespoons at a time, stirring until ice cream melts. Sprinkle with chocolate.
Yield: 4½ quarts punch

RUM BALLS

1 package (12 ounces) vanilla wafers
1 package (16 ounces) pecan pieces
½ cup honey
⅓ cup bourbon
⅓ cup dark rum
¼ cup vanilla wafer crumbs or ⅓ cup
    powdered sugar

Process vanilla wafers in food processor until crumbs are fine. Transfer to a large bowl. Process pecans in food processor until finely chopped. Stir into wafer crumbs. Stir in honey, bourbon, and rum.

Shape dough into 1-inch balls and roll in crumbs or powdered sugar. Place in an airtight container; store in refrigerator up to one week.
Yield: 6 dozen rum balls

CARAMEL-ALMOND TARTLETS

These petite tarts have a thick shortbread crust and a chewy caramel top.

1¼ cups all-purpose flour
2 tablespoons firmly packed brown sugar
¾ teaspoon salt
½ cup cold butter, cut into pieces
1 egg yolk
1 tablespoon whipping cream
1 teaspoon vanilla extract
¾ cup granulated sugar
¾ cup whipping cream
½ teaspoon almond extract
1 cup sliced almonds

*Y*ou'll love sinking your teeth into these chewy **Caramel-Almond Tartlets**! Add an extra measure of interest by using a variety of molds to shape them.

Process first 3 ingredients in a food processor just until blended. Add pieces of butter, pulsing 5 or 6 times or until mixture is crumbly.

Combine egg yolk, 1 tablespoon whipping cream, and vanilla; stir well. With processor running, slowly add egg mixture through food chute; process just until ingredients form a ball and leave sides of bowl. Shape dough into a flat disc; cover and chill 30 minutes.

Place ¾ cup granulated sugar in a large, heavy skillet. Cook over medium heat, stirring constantly with a wooden spoon, until sugar melts and syrup is golden. Remove from heat and slowly add ¾ cup whipping cream, stirring gently. (Sugar may crack and harden, but will melt again.) Return to heat and cook, stirring gently, until mixture is smooth and thickened. Remove from heat; stir in almond extract and almonds. Cool.

Cut chilled dough in half; divide each half into 8 balls. Press each ball into a lightly greased 1½-inch round tartlet pan; place tartlet pans on a baking sheet. Bake at 350° for 12 minutes. Cool slightly.

Increase oven temperature to 400°. Fill each tartlet shell with 1 tablespoon almond filling. Bake at 400° for 14 to 18 minutes or until golden. Cool completely on a wire rack. Remove from pans.
Yield: 16 tartlets
Note: For variety, we baked some of the tartlets in 4 x 2-inch barquette (boat-shaped) molds. We reduced the baking time for the crust and tartlets each to 9 minutes.

GINGERBREAD TRIFLE

Pair homemade gingerbread with custard and you get this fabulous dessert that can be made ahead. Bake the gingerbread and prepare the custard up to a day ahead, but wait until several hours before serving to mix them. For a shortcut, prepare gingerbread from a packaged mix. You can also use commercial vanilla pudding as a stand-in for our wonderfully thick custard.

½ cup butter or margarine, softened
½ cup firmly packed dark brown sugar
1 large egg
1 cup molasses
2½ cups all-purpose flour
1 tablespoon ground ginger
2 teaspoons baking powder
½ teaspoon baking soda
½ teaspoon salt
¼ teaspoon freshly ground pepper (optional)
1 cup hot water
　 Custard (recipe follows)
2 cups frozen whipped topping, thawed
4 English toffee-flavored candy bars
　　(1.4 ounces each), coarsely chopped

Beat butter at medium speed with an electric mixer until creamy. Gradually add sugar, beating until light and fluffy. Add egg and molasses, mixing well.

Combine flour and next 5 ingredients; add to butter mixture alternately with water, beginning and ending with flour mixture. Beat at low speed after each addition until blended. Pour batter into a greased 13 x 9-inch baking pan.

Bake at 350° for 30 to 35 minutes or until a wooden pick inserted in center comes out clean. Cool in pan on a wire rack.

Cut gingerbread into cubes. Arrange one-third of gingerbread cubes in a 3-quart trifle bowl; top with one-third of Custard. Repeat layers twice, ending with Custard. Cover and chill until ready to serve.

Before serving, spread whipped topping over trifle. Sprinkle with chopped candy bars.
Yield: 10 servings

CUSTARD

1⅓ cups sugar
⅔ cup all-purpose flour
½ teaspoon salt
5 cups milk
6 egg yolks, lightly beaten
1 tablespoon vanilla extract or dark rum

Combine first 3 ingredients in a large heavy saucepan; whisk in milk. Cook over medium heat, stirring constantly, until thickened and bubbly. Gradually stir about one-fourth of hot mixture into egg yolks; add to remaining hot mixture, stirring constantly. Cook over medium heat, stirring constantly, 3 minutes. Remove from heat; add vanilla or rum. Cool to room temperature. Assemble trifle or cover and chill custard until ready for assembly.
Yield: 5 cups custard

POINSETTIA SIPPERS

4 cups cranberry juice cocktail
4 cups apple juice
1 cup sugar
¼ cup orange juice
6 whole cloves
4 cinnamon sticks (3 inches each)
4 cups water
　 Garnish: orange rind curls and cinnamon sticks

Combine first 7 ingredients in a Dutch oven, stirring until sugar dissolves. Bring to a simmer; cover and cook 30 minutes. Remove cloves and cinnamon sticks from pan with a slotted spoon. Serve warm or chilled. Garnish, if desired.
Yield: 12 cups beverage
Note: You can add 1 cup vodka with first 7 ingredients for a Poinsettia Cocktail.

*P*oinsettia Sippers are a refreshingly delicious blend of fruit juices and spices. Garnish with orange rind curls and cinnamon sticks for a festive presentation.

SOUTHWESTERN GRILL OUT

Spice up your seasonal entertaining by hosting a Christmas cookout! Using the vibrant colors and bold flavors of the Southwest will heat up your outdoor gathering. Our menu of grilled specialties offers a delicious alternative to traditional Yuletide fare. ¡Viva the holidays!

ZINGY HERB TEA CIDER

A great warm-you-up drink.

  1 quart water
  6 Red Zinger® tea bags
 24 whole cloves
  1 orange
    Cheesecloth
 24 whole allspice
  2 cinnamon sticks (3 inches long each), broken
  5 cups apple cider
  5 cups cranberry juice drink
 ½ cup sugar
 1½ to 2 cups dark rum
    Cinnamon sticks to serve (optional)

Bring water to a boil; add tea bags. Remove from heat; cover and steep 5 minutes. Remove and discard tea bags.

Insert cloves into skin of orange. Cut a 6-inch square of cheesecloth; place allspice and broken cinnamon sticks in center and tie with string.

Combine tea, orange, spice bag, cider, cranberry juice, and sugar in a Dutch oven; bring to a boil. Cover, reduce heat, and simmer 1 hour. Remove from heat; cool to room temperature. Remove and discard orange and spice bag. (At this point, you can refrigerate mixture in a non-metal airtight container up to 3 days.)

To serve, combine cider mixture and rum in Dutch oven; cook over low heat until hot, stirring occasionally. Ladle cider into mugs; serve warm with cinnamon-stick stirrers, if desired.
Yield: 14 cups cider

GRILLED SHRIMP WITH BACON AND JALAPEÑOS

If you're in a hurry, try the fully cooked bacon slices. Don't use flat, thin wooden picks—use thick, round ones.

 16 thick, round wooden picks
 16 unpeeled, large fresh shrimp
  2 jalapeño peppers
  2 tablespoons olive oil
 ¼ teaspoon salt
 ⅛ teaspoon black pepper
  8 thick-cut bacon slices, halved

Soak round wooden picks in water 30 minutes.

Peel shrimp, leaving tails on; devein, if desired. Set shrimp aside.

Cut each jalapeño pepper lengthwise into 8 pieces; remove seeds.

Toss together shrimp, jalapeño peppers, olive oil, salt, and black pepper in a large bowl. Set aside.

Microwave bacon slices on HIGH 30 seconds.

Place 1 shrimp and 1 piece of jalapeño pepper together and wrap with 1 bacon piece. Secure with a wooden pick. Repeat procedure with remaining shrimp, jalapeño pepper pieces, and bacon slices.

Grill, covered, over medium-high heat (350° to 400°) for 4 to 6 minutes or until shrimp turn pink, turning once.
Yield: 8 servings

HOT SPICED FRUIT PUNCH

  6 cups cranberry-raspberry drink
  2 cups orange-strawberry-banana juice
  1 teaspoon whole allspice
  2 orange-and-spice tea bags
  5 lemon rind strips (about 3 inches long x ¾ inches wide each)
  1 cinnamon stick (3 inches long)
 ¼ cup sweetened dried cranberries
 ¼ cup diced dried apricots
  2 tablespoons sugar
    Cinnamon sticks to serve (optional)

Combine first 6 ingredients in a large saucepan; cover and cook mixture 30 minutes over medium-low heat. Remove from heat; let stand 30 minutes. Strain mixture; discard solids. Return juice mixture to pan; stir in cranberries, apricots, and sugar. Cook over medium-low heat 30 minutes, stirring occasionally. Ladle into mugs; serve with a cinnamon stick, if desired.
Yield: 8 cups punch

Get the party off to a great start by serving Grilled Shrimp with Bacon and Jalapeños. A warm and robust beverage, **Zingy Herb Tea Cider** is ideal for a Southwestern grill out.

LIME SOUP

 3 whole cloves
 1 to 2 teaspoons dried oregano
 1 cinnamon stick (3 inches long)
 4 cans (32 ounces each) chicken
    broth
 $^1/_2$ to $^2/_3$ cup fresh lime juice
 $^1/_2$ teaspoon salt
    Toppings: diced cooked
    chicken, diced avocado, lime
    wedges, fried tortilla chips,
    shredded Monterey Jack
    cheese

Cook first 3 ingredients in a large stockpot over medium-high heat 2 to 3 minutes, stirring constantly. Add broth, lime juice, and salt. Bring to a boil; reduce heat and simmer 1 to 2 minutes. Remove cloves and cinnamon stick. Serve with desired toppings.
Yield: Makes 4 quarts

Pair zesty Lime Soup with a wedge of delectable Jalapeño Cornbread and you've got one hot number! An outdoor oven is great for keeping the cornbread warm.

JALAPEÑO CORNBREAD

 1 cup self-rising cornmeal
 $^1/_2$ teaspoon baking soda
 $^1/_4$ teaspoon salt
 1$^1/_2$ cups (6 ounces) shredded Cheddar cheese
 1 cup milk
 3 large eggs, lightly beaten
 1 can (8.25 ounces) whole kernel corn,
    drained
 $^1/_2$ cup chopped onion
 1 jar (2 ounces) diced pimiento, drained
 3 tablespoons bacon drippings
 3 jalapeño peppers, seeded and chopped
 1 teaspoon garlic powder

Combine first 3 ingredients in a large bowl; add cheese and remaining ingredients, stirring just until dry ingredients are moistened. Spoon batter into a greased 10-inch cast-iron skillet. Bake at 350° for 45 minutes or until golden.
Yield: 10 servings

For a deliciously colorful presentation, serve hearty Mesquite-Smoked Pork with Texas Caviar. The black-eyed pea mixture is a popular regional dish that's surprisingly savory. Chipotle Potato Gratin and Grilled Marinated Vegetables round out the meal.

GRILLED MARINATED VEGETABLES

These veggies taste great if you want to serve them hot from the grill, but they develop even more flavor if marinated overnight.

- ¹/₃ cup white balsamic vinegar
- 2 tablespoons olive oil
- 2 shallots, finely chopped
- 1¹/₂ teaspoons molasses
- 1 teaspoon dried Italian seasoning
- ¹/₄ teaspoon salt
- ¹/₄ teaspoon black pepper
- ¹/₂ pound carrots
- 2 large red bell peppers
- 2 large yellow bell peppers
- 2 large onions

Combine first 7 ingredients in a large bowl. Set aside.

Cut carrots and remaining vegetables into large pieces. Add vegetables to vinegar mixture, tossing to coat. Let stand 30 minutes, stirring occasionally. Drain vegetables, reserving vinegar mixture. Arrange vegetables in a grill basket.

Grill over direct, medium-high heat until crisp-tender, 10 to 15 minutes, turning occasionally. Serve immediately or return vegetables to reserved vinegar mixture, tossing gently. Cover and refrigerate 8 hours.

Yield: 8 servings

MESQUITE-SMOKED PORK WITH TEXAS CAVIAR

1 cup frozen black-eyed peas
1 cup water
$^1/_3$ cup seeded, chopped fresh tomato
$^1/_4$ cup chopped yellow bell pepper
$^1/_4$ cup chopped green bell pepper
$^1/_4$ cup chopped onion
$^1/_4$ cup Italian dressing
1 tablespoon chopped fresh parsley
2 teaspoons seeded, minced jalapeño pepper
$^1/_4$ teaspoon minced garlic
$^1/_8$ teaspoon black pepper
$^1/_8$ teaspoon ground cumin
  Mesquite chips
  Cooking spray
1 center rib pork roast (8 ribs and about 4 pounds)
8 garlic cloves, minced
$^1/_2$ teaspoon salt
$^1/_2$ teaspoon coarsely ground black pepper

Combine peas and water. Bring to a boil. Cover, reduce heat, and simmer 35 minutes or until tender. Drain; let cool. Combine peas, tomato, and next 9 ingredients in a medium bowl, stirring well. Cover and chill at least 2 hours.

Soak mesquite chips in water 30 minutes; drain. Wrap in heavy-duty aluminum foil; make several holes in foil.

Light gas grill on one side; place foil-wrapped chips directly on hot lava rocks. Remove grill rack from unlighted side of grill. Coat grill rack with cooking spray. Place rack over cool lava rocks; let grill preheat to medium-hot (350° to 400°) 10 to 15 minutes.

Trim fat from roast. Mash 8 garlic cloves, salt, and $^1/_2$ teaspoon black pepper to a paste. Rub surface of roast with garlic paste. Coat roast with cooking spray. Insert meat thermometer into thickest part of roast, if desired, making sure it does not touch bone or fat.

Place roast on rack opposite hot lava rocks. Grill, covered, $1^1/_2$ hours or until meat thermometer registers 150°. Remove roast from grill. Cover with aluminum foil; let stand 15 minutes or until thermometer registers 160°. Carve roast into 8 chops and serve with chilled black-eyed pea mixture.
Yield: 6 to 8 servings
Note: To use a charcoal grill, prepare black-eyed pea mixture and soak mesquite chips as directed. Remove grill rack. Pile charcoal on each side of grill, leaving center empty. Place a drip pan between coals. Prepare fire; let burn 10 to 15 minutes. Place chips directly on hot coals. Coat grill rack with cooking spray and place over coals. Prepare roast as directed, inserting meat thermometer into thickest part of roast, if desired. Place roast on rack over drip pan. Grill, covered, $1^1/_2$ hours or until meat thermometer registers 150°. Remove roast from grill. Cover with aluminum foil and let stand 15 minutes or until thermometer registers 160°.

CHIPOTLE POTATO GRATIN

Canned chipotle peppers in adobo sauce add a smoky flavor to this two-potato casserole.

1 garlic clove, minced
1 cup whipping cream
1 cup milk
$1^1/_2$ tablespoons all-purpose flour
2 teaspoons adobo sauce
1 teaspoon mashed chipotle pepper
$^1/_4$ teaspoon salt
$^1/_4$ teaspoon black pepper
2 medium-size sweet potatoes, peeled and thinly sliced
1 medium-size baking potato, peeled and thinly sliced

Sprinkle garlic in bottom of a buttered 11 x 7-inch baking dish.

Whisk together whipping cream and next 6 ingredients.

Layer half of sweet and baking potato slices over garlic; top with half of cream mixture. Repeat procedure with remaining potato slices and cream mixture.

Bake, covered, at 350° for 40 minutes. Uncover and bake 30 more minutes or until gratin is golden brown. Let stand 15 minutes before serving.
Yield: 6 to 8 servings

SLOW-COOKER QUESO BLANCO

Ask the deli to slice white American cheese for you. Then just roughly tear the slices and place them in the slow cooker.

1 small onion, diced
3 garlic cloves, minced
1 can (14½ ounces) petite-cut diced tomatoes, drained
1 cup milk
¾ cup pickled jalapeño slices, minced
1 can (4.5 ounces) chopped green chiles, undrained
1 tablespoon juice from jalapeño slices
1 teaspoon ground cumin
½ teaspoon dried oregano
½ teaspoon coarsely ground black pepper
2 pounds deli white American cheese, sliced
  Tortilla chips to serve

Place onion in a medium microwave-safe bowl; cover loosely with heavy-duty plastic wrap. Microwave on HIGH 2 minutes. Stir in garlic and next 8 ingredients.

Roughly tear cheese slices; place in a 4-quart slow cooker. Pour onion mixture over cheese.

Cover and cook on LOW 2 hours. Stir gently to blend ingredients. Serve with tortilla chips.
Yield: 6½ cups dip
Note: This big-batch dip freezes well. Spoon into serving-size freezer containers and freeze up to 1 month. Thaw overnight in refrigerator. Reheat in microwave on MEDIUM.

PINEAPPLE FLAN

½ cup sugar
1 can (14 ounces) sweetened condensed milk
1 cup whipping cream
½ cup pineapple juice
3 large eggs
3 egg yolks
1 teaspoon vanilla extract
1 cup finely chopped fresh pineapple

Sprinkle sugar in an 8-inch round cake pan; place over medium heat and cook, shaking pan constantly, until sugar melts and turns a light golden brown. Remove from heat.

Process condensed milk and next 5 ingredients in a blender until smooth, stopping to scrape down sides; stir in pineapple. Pour mixture over caramelized sugar in pan. Cover with aluminum foil; place in a roasting pan. Pour hot water into roasting pan to a depth of 1 inch.

Bake at 350° for 1 hour and 10 minutes or until just barely set. Remove cake pan from water and uncover; cool flan completely in cake pan on a wire rack. Cover and chill for at least 8 hours.

Run a knife around edge of flan to loosen; invert onto a serving plate. Cut into wedges to serve.
Yield: 6 servings

FIRESIDE COFFEE

You can easily make a non-alcoholic version of this after-dinner warmer by substituting hot coffee for the bourbon.

2 cups half-and-half
2 squares (1 ounce each) unsweetened baking chocolate, chopped
2 cups hot brewed coffee
¾ cup bourbon
½ to 1 cup sugar
⅔ cup whipping cream
1 teaspoon vanilla extract
   Whipped cream to serve (optional)

Microwave half-and-half in a 2-cup glass measuring cup on HIGH 1 to 2 minutes or until steamy. Pour over chocolate; let stand 1 minute and whisk until combined. Stir in coffee and next 4 ingredients; pour into cups and serve with a dollop of whipped cream, if desired. Serve immediately.
Yield: 8 six-ounce servings
Note: Recipe can be multiplied as desired to serve more.

Set out this Pineapple Flan and watch it disappear! The temptingly rich custard is sure to please even the most discriminating palate.

Mocha Torte, iced with *Mocha Frosting*, offers a sweet ending to a festive evening. A toasty, after-dinner drink, **Fireside Coffee** is a tasty complement to dessert.

MOCHA TORTE

1¼ cups hot water
¼ cup instant coffee granules, divided
1 package (18.25 ounces) devil's food cake mix with pudding
1 cup butter or margarine, softened
2 cups powdered sugar
2 tablespoons cocoa
2 tablespoons whipping cream
¼ cup coffee liqueur (optional)
Mocha Frosting (recipe follows)

Stir together water and 2 tablespoons coffee granules until granules dissolve.

Prepare cake mix according to package directions, substituting coffee mixture for water. Pour into 3 greased and floured 8-inch round cake pans.

Bake at 350° for 18 minutes or until a wooden pick inserted in center comes out clean. Cool in pans on wire racks 10 to 15 minutes; remove from pans and cool on wire racks.

Beat butter at medium speed with an electric mixer until creamy; gradually add powdered sugar, beating at low speed until blended. Add remaining 2 tablespoons coffee granules, cocoa, and whipping cream, beating until blended.

Brush cake layers evenly with coffee liqueur, if desired. Spread cocoa mixture between cake layers. Spread Mocha Frosting on top and sides of cake.

Yield: one 3-layer cake

MOCHA FROSTING

3 cups powdered sugar
¼ cup cocoa
2 tablespoons instant coffee granules
½ cup butter or margarine, softened
1 tablespoon vanilla extract
1 tablespoon coffee liqueur (see Note)

Stir together first 3 ingredients. Beat butter at medium speed with an electric mixer until creamy; gradually add powdered sugar mixture, beating until spreading consistency. Stir in vanilla and coffee liqueur.

Yield: 3 cups frosting

Note: You can substitute 1 tablespoon whipping cream for the liqueur.

project INSTRUCTIONS

Making your Christmas a magical experience is easy! Just follow these step-by-step instructions to fashion original decorations and gifts that will be enjoyed for years to come. Also see the General Instructions on page 185 for additional tips, hints, and how-tos.

CELEBRATING 20 YEARS OF SIGHTS

KEEPSAKE ORNAMENT
(shown on page 6)

You will need tracing paper, craft knife and cutting mat, mat board, poster board, spray adhesive, purple foil origami paper, green and orange acrylic paints, paintbrushes, craft glue, silver and lime glitter, and linen thread.

Use spray adhesive in a well-ventilated area.

1. Use the patterns, page 178, and cut one ornament piece each from mat board and poster board.
2. Spray one side of each small piece with adhesive; apply foil paper and trim the edges. Paint one side of each medium and large piece; allow to dry.
3. Draw the year with craft glue on the foil side of each small piece and spray the painted side of each medium piece with adhesive. Sprinkle the pieces with glitter, allow to dry, and shake off the excess.
4. Spray the back of each ornament piece with adhesive. Fold a 24" thread length in half. Layer the pieces as shown, sandwiching the thread between the pieces with the loop at the top. Knot and trim the thread ends at the bottom.

BERIBBONED ORNAMENT
(shown on page 7)

You will need a 3¹/₂" dia. glass ornament, craft knife, assorted ribbons and/or trims, hot glue gun, 1¹/₄" dia. silver jingle bell, ³/₄" dia. flat bead, numeral stickers, cream cardstock, two self-adhesive clear tags, and liquid fray preventative.

1. Remove the ornament end cap. Use the craft knife to enlarge the opening in the end cap; set aside.
2. Cut five 20" ribbon lengths; set one aside.
3. With the centers at the bottom, glue the ribbon lengths up the sides of the ornament as shown.
4. Thread the jingle bell onto the center of the reserved ribbon and the ribbon ends through the bead. Glue the bead to the bottom of the ornament. Glue the ribbon up the sides of the ornament.
5. Thread the ribbon ends through the opening in the cap; carefully replace the end cap.
6. Adhere the stickers to the cardstock; cut out close to the stickers. Sandwich the cardstock between the tags. Attach the tag to the ornament.
7. Tie a ribbon hanger through the end cap. Trim, then apply fray preventative to all ribbon ends.

SNOWFLAKE PILLOW ORNAMENT
(shown on page 7)

You will need light purple fabric; disappearing ink marker; beading needle and thread; 1.5mm light purple bugle beads, 8mm clear flower beads, assorted light and dark purple seed beads, clear leaf beads, clear heart beads, and a 12mm clear flat bead; and ¹/₈" dia. light purple cording.

Thread the needle with one doubled strand of thread for all beading.

1. Cut two 5" fabric squares.
2. On the right side of one square, find the center; then, use the marker to draw a six-point starburst with 1¹/₄"-long spokes.
3. For each spoke, bring the needle up at the center and thread 20 bugle, 1 flower, and 1 seed bead onto the needle; go back down through the flower and fabric; knot the thread ends. Halfway down the spoke, thread 2 bugle, 1 leaf, and 1 seed bead onto the needle; go down through the fabric and knot the thread ends. Repeat on the remaining side of the spoke.
4. Between each spoke, thread 1 bugle, 1 heart, and 2 seed beads onto the needle; go down through the fabric and knot the thread ends.

5. For the snowflake center, thread the clear flat bead and a purple seed bead onto the needle. Go back down through the flat bead and fabric and knot the thread ends.
6. For the hanger, tack the ends of a 5" cording length to the right side of one square.
7. Matching the right sides, leaving an opening for turning, and using a 1/2" seam allowance, sew the squares together. Trim the corners, turn right side out, and sew the opening closed.

WOOD BURNED STAR
(shown on page 7)

You will need fine-grit sandpaper, 2²/₃"h x 3¹/₂" dia. wooden ornament, tack cloth, tracing paper, transfer paper, wood burning tool, metallic gold rub-on finish, and red wire-edged ribbon.

1. Sand, then wipe the ornament with the tack cloth.
2. Trace the star pattern, page 159, onto tracing paper; then, transfer the pattern onto the ornament.
3. Follow the manufacturer's instructions to lightly burn the wood along the transferred lines.
4. Leaving the burned area unfinished, apply gold finish to the ornament. Buff the ornament to the desired sheen.
5. Hang the ornament from a ribbon bow.

FROSTED BALL WITH BEADED COLLAR
(shown on page 7)

You will need a 3¹/₄" dia. frosted glass ball ornament; beading thread; beading needle; liquid fray

preventative; the following beads: eight 5mm crystal bicone, 384 clear and silver-lined seed, 252 silver seed, eight 5mm crystal teardrop, and four 5mm opalescent round beads; and sheer white ribbon.

Refer to Beading Basics, page 185, and Collar Beading Diagrams, page 123, to complete each row of the collar. Using 1¹/₂-yard strands, thread the needle with one doubled strand of thread to begin, adding new thread as needed.

The number of beads may need to be adjusted as sizes may vary within a package.

1. For Row 1, leaving a 3" tail and locking the first bead in place, thread 1 bicone bead and 10 assorted seed beads. Repeat the beading pattern three more times. Thread the needle through the locking bead twice to secure Row 1; place on the ornament.
2. For Row 2, thread 25 silver seed beads; then, thread the needle through the next bicone bead in Row 1 to complete the scallop. Repeat the beading pattern three more times.
3. For Row 3, thread 18 assorted seed beads, 1 teardrop bead, and 18 assorted seed beads; then, thread the needle through the next bicone bead in Row 1 to complete the scallop. Repeat the beading pattern three more times. Thread the needle through the next 18 assorted seed beads and the teardrop bead in Row 3.
4. For Row 4, thread 14 silver seed beads, 1 bicone bead, and 14 silver seed beads; then, thread the needle through the next teardrop bead in Row 3. Repeat the beading pattern three more times.
5. For Row 5, thread 25 assorted seed beads; then, thread the needle through the next bicone bead in Row 4. Thread 10 silver seed beads, 1 round bead, and 1 teardrop bead;

double back though the round bead, silver seed beads, and bicone bead. Thread 25 assorted seed beads; then, thread the needle through the next teardrop bead in Row 3. Repeat the beading pattern three more times.
6. Thread the needle through the first seed bead in Row 5 twice to lock in place. Secure the thread ends to complete the collar.
7. Thread a ribbon hanger through the ornament end cap.

EMBROIDERED BIRD ORNAMENT
(shown on page 8)

You will need tissue paper; two 8" light teal felt squares; light green, dark green, teal, dark teal, and dark brown 3-ply Persian wool yarn; crewel embroidery needle; pearl seed beads, beading thread, and a beading needle; polyester fiberfill; and clear nylon thread.

Refer to Embroidery, page 185, before beginning the project. Use one ply of yarn for all embroidery.

1. Trace the bird design, page 159, onto tissue. Center and pin the pattern on one felt square. Follow the stitching key, page 159, to embroider the design. Carefully tear away the paper. Sew on beads.
2. With the squares together, cut out the bird 1" outside the design.
3. Matching the right sides and leaving an opening for turning, use a 1/2" seam allowance to sew the pieces together. Trim the seam allowance to 1/4". Clip the curves, turn right side out, and stuff with fiberfill. Sew the opening closed.
4. For the hanger, attach a 10" nylon thread length through the top of the ornament.

SCHERENSCHNITTE TREE

(shown on page 11)

You will need parchment paper, sharp pencil, transparent tape, small sharp scissors, sharp needle, and ecru thread.

1. Fold the parchment paper in half; unfold. Trace the pattern half, page 161, twice onto the parchment, aligning the blue line on the pattern with the fold line on the paper. Refold; tape the paper edges together.
2. Carefully cut out the trees.
3. Use the needle to pierce a hole through each dot on the tree.
4. Unfold each tree and erase the pencil marks. Match the fold lines and machine stitch the trees together along the fold, leaving an 8" tail at the top. Knot the thread ends for the hanger.

LOVE PILLOW ORNAMENT

(shown on page 8)

You will need tissue paper, plain and crushed velvet, fabric glue, beading needle and thread, gold seed beads, polyester fiberfill, iridescent seed beads, and 4mm luster beads.

1. Use the flap pattern, page 159, and cut a plain velvet flap. Cut a 5¹⁄₂" x 8" crushed velvet piece for the pillow.
2. Glue the flap edges adjacent to the point ¹⁄₄" to the wrong side. Allow to dry.
3. Trace the "Love" pattern, page 159, onto tissue; cut out ¹⁄₂" outside the word. Pin the pattern to the center right side of the flap.

4. Sew the gold beads to the flap along the pattern lines; carefully tear away the tissue paper.
5. Matching the wrong side of the flap to the right side of the pillow piece, baste the flap along the top edge. With the flap between the layers and matching the short ends, fold the pillow piece in half. Using a ¹⁄₄" seam allowance and leaving an opening for turning, sew the edges together. Turn the pillow right side out. Stuff the pillow; sew the opening closed.
6. Take a small stitch along the edge at one end of the flap. Alternating gold and iridescent beads, thread 7 seed beads, 1 luster bead, and 7 seed beads onto the needle. Take a small stitch on the flap edge ³⁄₄" from the first. Repeat to make three more scallops.
7. Thread beads onto the needle for the desired tassel length. Run the thread around the last bead and back up through the beads on the strand. Take a small stitch on the flap edge. Repeat to make two more strands.
8. Repeat Step 6 along the remaining edge of the flap. Knot and trim the thread.

JOY REDWORK ORNAMENT

(shown on page 8)

You will need vinegar, red embroidery floss, red iron-on transfer pencil, tracing paper, two 10" squares of bleached muslin, embroidery needle, four ¹⁄₂" dia. red buttons, polyester fiberfill, and ¹⁄₄"w red grosgrain ribbon.

Refer to Embroidery, page 185, before beginning the project. Use two strands of floss for all embroidery.

1. Mix 1 tablespoon vinegar in 8 ounces of clear water. Soak the floss in the mixture to release the excess dye. Allow to dry.

2. Use the transfer pencil to trace the pattern, page 161, onto tracing paper. Follow manufacturer's instructions to transfer the pattern to the center of one muslin square.
3. Embroider the design.
4. Sew one button to each corner of the design. Matching right sides and leaving an opening for turning, sew the squares together ¹⁄₂" from the design. Trim the corners; turn right side out.
5. Lightly stuff the ornament. Sew the opening closed. Sew a ribbon hanger to the back and a bow to the front.

CROCHETED ANGEL

(shown on page 8)

Refer to Knit and Crochet, page 186, for abbreviations.

You will need bedspread weight (#10) white cotton thread, steel crochet hook size 6 (1.80), 1" plastic ring, ³⁄₈"w silver ribbon, needle, white thread, and nine 4mm silver beads.

JOINING WITH SC

When instructed to join with sc, begin with a slip knot on the hook. Insert the hook in a stitch or space as indicated. YO and pull up a loop, YO and draw through both loops on the hook.

HEAD

Rnd 1 (Right side): Join thread to plastic ring with sc; work 40 **more** sc in ring; join with sl st to first sc: 41 sc.
Note: Mark last round as right side.
Neck: Ch 1, turn; sc in same st and in next 8 sc, leave remaining 32 sc unworked; do **not** finish off: 9 sc.

RIGHT WING

Row 1: Ch 14, dc in sixth ch from hook, ch 1, skip next ch, ★ dc in next ch, ch 1, skip next ch; repeat from ★ 2 times **more**, sc in last ch; with **right** side facing, sl st in first sc on Neck.

Row 2: Ch 1, turn; sc in first sc, ch 1 (dc in next dc, ch 1) 4 times, skip next ch, dc in next ch: 5 ch-1 sps.

Row 3: Ch 4 (counts as first dc plus ch-1, now and throughout), turn; (dc in next dc, ch 1) 4 times, sc in last sc, sl st in **same** sc on Neck.

Row 4: Ch 1, turn; sc in first sc, (ch 1, dc in next dc) across.

Row 5: Ch 4, turn; (dc in next dc, ch 1) 4 times, sc in last sc, sl st in **next** sc on Neck.

Row 6: Repeat Row 4.

Row 7: Repeat Row 3.

Row 8: Repeat Row 4.

Row 9: Repeat Row 5; finish off.

DRESS

Row 1: With **right** side facing, join thread with sl st in first dc on Row 9 of Right Wing; ch 23, dc in sixth ch from hook, ch 1, skip next ch, (dc in next ch, ch 1, skip next ch) 8 times; working in sts across Row 9, (dc in next ch, ch 1) 5 times, sc in last sc, sl st in same sc on Neck: 15 sps.

Row 2: Ch 1, turn; sc in first sc, ch 1, (dc in next dc, ch 1) 14 times, skip next ch, dc in next ch: 15 dc and 15 ch-1 sps.

Row 3: Ch 4, turn; (dc in next dc, ch 1) 14 times, sc in last sc, sl st in **next** sc on Neck.

Row 4: Ch 1, turn; sc in first sc, (ch 1, dc in next dc) across.

Row 5: Ch 4, turn; (dc in next dc, ch 1) 14 times, sc in last sc, sl st in **same** sc on Neck.

Row 6: Ch 1, turn; sc in first sc, (ch 1, dc in next dc) across.

Rows 7-17: Repeat Rows 3-6 twice, then repeat Rows 3-5 once **more**. Finish off.

LEFT WING

Row 1: With **right** side facing, skip first 10 dc on Row 17 of Dress and join with sl st in next dc; place marker around dc just worked into for Edging placement, ch 4, (dc in next dc, ch 1) 4 times, sc in last sc, sl st in **next** sc on Neck: 5 ch-1 sps.

Row 2: Ch 1, turn; sc in first sc, (ch 1, dc in next dc) across.

Row 3: Ch 4, turn; (dc in next dc, ch 1) 4 times, sc in last sc, sl st in **same** sc on Neck.

Row 4: Ch 1, turn; sc in first sc, (ch 1, dc in next dc) across.

Row 5: Ch 4, turn; (dc in next dc, ch 1) 4 times, sc in last sc, sl st in **next** sc on Neck.

Rows 6-9: Repeat Rows 2 and 3 twice. Finish off.

EDGING

To work Cluster: Ch 3, YO, insert hook in third ch from hook, YO and pull up a loop, YO and draw through 2 loops on hook, YO, insert hook in same ch, YO and pull up a loop, YO and draw through 2 loops on hook, YO and draw through all 3 loops on hook.

With **right** side facing, join with sl st in marked dc on Dress; ch 2, dc in same st, (sl st, ch 2, dc) in top of dc at end of first 8 rows on Left Wing; working in sts across Row 9, (sl st, ch 2, hdc) in first 5 dc, sl st in last sc; working in unworked scs on Head, sl st in first 3 scs, work Cluster, (skip next 2 sc, dc in next sc, work Cluster) 8 times, skip next 2 sc, sl st in last 3 sc; working in free loops of beginning ch on Right Wing, (sl st, ch 2, hdc) in first ch (opposite sc), skip next ch, ★ (sl st, ch 2, hdc) in next ch, skip next ch; repeat from ★ 3 times **more**, (sl st, ch 2, dc) in next ch; (sl st, ch 2, dc) in top of dc at end of first 8 rows on Right Wing, sl st in top of dc at end of last row, ch 2; working in free loops of beginning ch on Row 1 of Dress, skip first ch, (sl st in next ch, ch 2, skip next ch) 9 times, (sl st, ch 2, dc) in next ch; (sl st, ch 2, dc) in top of dc at end of first 16 rows on Dress, sl st in top of dc at end of last row, ch 2; working in sts across Row 17, (sl st in next dc, ch 2) 9 times; join with sl st to joining sl st. Finish off.

ANGEL FINISHING

1. Weave the ribbon through spaces on Row 1 of Dress and every other row. Weave the ribbon through spaces next to Edging on Wings; use the needle and thread to secure all the ribbon ends.

2. Tie an 8" ribbon length into a bow. Sew the bow and the beads to the Angel.

MADONNA AND CHILD
(shown on page 9)

You will need a permanent pen; 6" x 8" piece of Aleene's® Clear Shrink-It™ Plastic; iridescent black dimensional paint; decoupage glue; cream, dark red, purple, light aqua, and aqua tissue paper; paintbrushes; gold rub-on metallic finish; lo-temp glue gun; and ³/₄ yd of ³/₁₆"w gold cord.

Use decoupage glue unless otherwise indicated.

1. Trace the pattern, page 161, onto the plastic. Paint over the grey lines with dimensional paint.

2. Referring to the photo for color placement, cut and decoupage tissue shapes to the back of the plastic.

3. For the gold areas, follow manufacturer's instructions and brush several coats of metallic finish on the back of the plastic.

4. Cut out the design.

5. Beginning at the top, hot glue the cord along the front edges of the ornament, looping the cord at the top to form the hanger.

POINSETTIA ANGEL

(shown on page 9)

You will need wire cutters, white silk poinsettia with largest petals approx. 4³/₄" long, 3" dia. foam half-ball, hot glue gun, 3"h porcelain doll head with 1¹/₂" long arms, gold glitter acrylic paint, paintbrush, chenille stem, 13" of 1¹/₂"w ivory satin ribbon, fabric glue, 14" x 16" ivory satin piece, 13" of 8¹/₂"w ivory pregathered lace, 1¹/₂ yds of 2¹/₄"w and ³/₄ yd of 1¹/₄"w sheer wire-edged ribbon, ³/₄ yd of ³/₁₆" dia. gold twisted cord, and gold craft wire.

Use fabric glue for all gluing unless otherwise noted.

1. For the angel body, cut and discard the center from the stem; then, cut the stem to 4". Refer to Fig. 1 and insert the stem into the half-ball (the flat side is the back of the body).

Fig. 1

2. Hot glue the doll head on the stem.
3. Lightly paint petals and doll hair gold; allow to dry.
4. For the arms, hot glue one end of a 6" chenille stem length into each doll arm. Folding the ends ¹/₂" to the wrong side, cover the arms with an 8" satin ribbon length. Hot glue the center of the arms to the back of the shoulders.

5. For the shawl, wrap and glue the remaining satin ribbon around shoulders.
6. For the skirt, press one long edge of the fabric 1" to the wrong side. Matching the wrong sides and short edges, fold the fabric in half (this fold is at the skirt bottom). Baste the lace to the top of the skirt. Pull the thread tightly to gather; knot the thread and trim the ends. Place the skirt around the poinsettia stem. Glue the raw fabric edges between the pressed edges at the back of the skirt.
7. For the wings, tie 2¹/₄"w ribbon into an 8"w bow; hot glue the bow to the top center skirt back and trim the ends.
8. For the scarf, wrap the center of the 1¹/₄"w ribbon around the head, crossing the ribbon just below the shawl. Hot glue a 3"w cord bow to the crossed ribbon; knot the ends.
9. For the hanger, bend a 6" wire length into a hook shape; hot glue to the ornament back.

FOLK-ART APPLIQUÉD ORNAMENT

(shown on page 9)

You will need dark yellow, black, blue, green, and red 100% wool fabrics; tracing paper; fabric glue; pinking shears; and coordinating embroidery floss.

Allow glue to dry after each application. Refer to Embroidery, page 185, before beginning the project. Use three strands of floss for all embroidery.

1. To felt wool, machine wash the fabrics separately in hot water, rinse in cold water, and dry in a hot dryer.
2. Use the patterns, page 160, and cut the background from black wool and the appliqués from blue and green wool. Glue the appliqués to the background.

3. Glue the background to red wool. Use pinking shears to cut ¹/₄" outside the background.
4. Work *Blanket Stitches* along the edges of the appliqués and background. Add *Stem Stitch* stems and a *French Knot* eye.
5. Follow Step 3 to add a dark yellow background layer.
6. For the hanger, attach a 5" floss length through the top of ornament.

CROCHETED SNOWFLAKE

(shown on page 9)

Refer to Knit and Crochet, page 186, for abbreviations.

You will need approx. 8 yds of bedspread weight cotton thread; steel crochet hook, size 5 (1.90 mm) **or** size needed for gauge; fabric stiffener; tracing paper; plastic wrap; ironing board; and stainless steel pins.

Gauge:
38 chs = 4" (10 cm)

SNOWFLAKE
Ch 6; join with sl st to form a ring.
Rnd 1: ★ Ch 20, sl st in ring, ch 26, sl st in 20ᵗʰ ch from hook, (ch 20, sl st in same ch) twice, ch 6, sl st in ring; repeat from ★ 5 times **more**; finish off.

FINISHING
1. Wash the snowflake and dry flat.
2. Follow manufacturer's instructions to work the stiffener into the snowflake.
3. Trace the pattern, page 160; leaving 1" around the design, cut it out. Stack the pattern and plastic wrap on the ironing board.
4. Place the snowflake right side up over the pattern. Pin the snowflake to fit the pattern; allow to dry.

SCHERENSCHNITTE REINDEER

(shown on page 11)

You will need tracing paper, transfer paper, black paper, small sharp scissors, craft glue stick, parchment paper, craft glue, small twigs, and jute twine.

1. Trace the patterns, page 163, onto tracing paper. Transfer the designs to black paper.
2. Carefully cut out the designs.
3. Use the glue stick to glue the designs to a 3" x 4³/₄" parchment piece. Use craft glue to glue twigs around the edges of the parchment. Tie twine around the twigs at the intersections and tie one end of a twine hanger to each of the top corners.

PENGUIN

(shown on page 10)

You will need black, white, and orange acrylic paints; paintbrushes; 3"h papier-mâché egg; tracing paper; ¹/₄ yd red flannel; paper-backed fusible web; hot glue gun; ¹/₂" dia. white pom-pom; utility scissors; two jumbo wooden craft sticks; wood tone spray; two bamboo skewers; and two black spoke sequins.

Allow paint to dry after each application. Use wood tone spray in a well-ventilated area.

1. Paint the egg as shown.
2. Refer to *Making Patterns*, page 185, and trace the patterns, page 160, onto tracing paper; cut out. Cut a flannel hat. Fuse two 2" x 4" flannel pieces together; cut out two mittens.

3. Matching right sides and curved edges, fold the hat in half. Use a ¹/₄" seam allowance and sew the curved edges together. Baste ¹/₄" from the top of the hat. Pull the threads tightly to gather; knot and trim the ends. Turn the hat right side out.
4. Fold and press the bottom of the hat for the cuff. Glue the hat to the penguin and the pom-pom to the hat.
5. For the skis, trim one end of each craft stick to a point. Apply wood tone spray.
6. For each pole, cut 4" from the pointed end of one skewer. Paint ³/₄" of the cut end black. Glue a sequin on the pointed end.
7. Glue the mittens, skis, and poles to the penguin.

SANTA ORNAMENT

(shown on page 10)

You will need tracing paper; two red and one white 7" x 10" felt pieces; disappearing ink marker; green, black, and pink felt scraps; craft glue; ¹/₃ yd black, ²/₃ yd red, and 1 yd white string sequins; 2" of ¹/₈"w flat gold braid; two 4mm black half-round beads; ¹/₄" dia. red bead; ¹/₂" dia. white pom-pom; and polyester fiberfill.

Allow glue to dry after each application.

1. Trace the patterns, page 164, onto tracing paper; cut out.
2. Stack the red felt pieces. Use the marker to draw around the body pattern on the top piece. Sew the pieces together on the drawn line. Cutting close to the stitching line, cut out the body.

3. Use the patterns and cut the remaining pieces from felt. Glue the pieces to the body.
4. Glue sequins to the ornament as shown.
5. For the belt buckle, glue four ¹/₂" braid pieces to the center of the belt in a buckle shape.
6. Glue the beads to the face for the eyes and nose. Glue the pom-pom to the hat.
7. Cut a 2"-long slit through the center back only. Lightly stuff Santa; sew the opening closed.

GLORY TO GOD

(shown on page 10)

You will need embroidery floss (see color key, page 162) and an 8" square of raw Belfast linen (32 ct).

1. To add support to stitches when working on linen, place the first Cross Stitch on the fabric with stitch 1-2 beginning and ending where a vertical fabric thread crosses over a horizontal fabric thread (Fig. 1).

Fig. 1

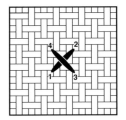

Using two strands of floss and working over two fabric threads, follow the chart and color key, page 162, to Cross Stitch the design.
2. Finish as desired (we made ours into a pillow ornament).

HANGING TIN STAR
(shown on page 10)

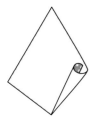

You will need tracing paper, utility scissors, 8" x 10" piece of aluminum flashing, needlenose pliers, ruler, heavy-duty craft glue, grey and black flat spray paints, fine steel wool, ½" dia. mirror, and fishing line.

Use caution when cutting and handling flashing. Use spray paint in a well-ventilated area and allow to dry after each application.

1. Use the patterns, page 162, and cut five of each diamond from flashing. Cut a 1¼" and a 1" flashing circle.
2. Use the pliers to crimp the edge of the small circle and the long edges of the diamonds.
3. Use the pliers to curl the uncrimped edges of each large diamond (Figs. 1a and 1b).

Fig. 1a   **Fig. 1b**

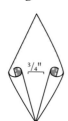

4. Center the ruler lengthwise on each small diamond and fold the flashing to a 45 degree angle.

5. Alternating sizes, glue the diamonds to the large circle (Figs. 2a and 2b).

Fig. 2a

Fig. 2b

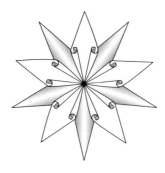

6. Glue the small circle to the center front of the star.
7. Lightly spray the star front with grey, then black. Use steel wool to remove the paint in places.
8. Glue the mirror to the center front of the star. Glue a fishing line hanger to the back of the star.

SANTA DOOR HANGER
(shown on page 11)

You will need an 8" x 10" piece of 18-mesh needlepoint canvas, masking tape, Paternayan Persian yarn (see color key, page 163), and a #24 tapestry needle.

1. Cover the canvas edges with masking tape.
2. Center and work the design on pages 162–163, using 1 strand of yarn and Tent Stitches (below).
3. Block the stitched piece and finish as desired (we made ours into a pillow door hanger).

Tent Stitches
Work a tent stitch to correspond to each square on the chart. When working a single row of Tent Stitches horizontally, vertically, or diagonally, use the Continental method (Fig. 1). When working an area having several rows of stitches, use the Basketweave method (Fig. 2).

Fig. 1

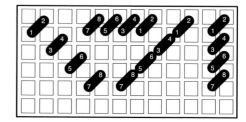

Fig. 2

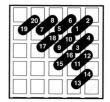

COLLAR BEADING DIAGRAMS

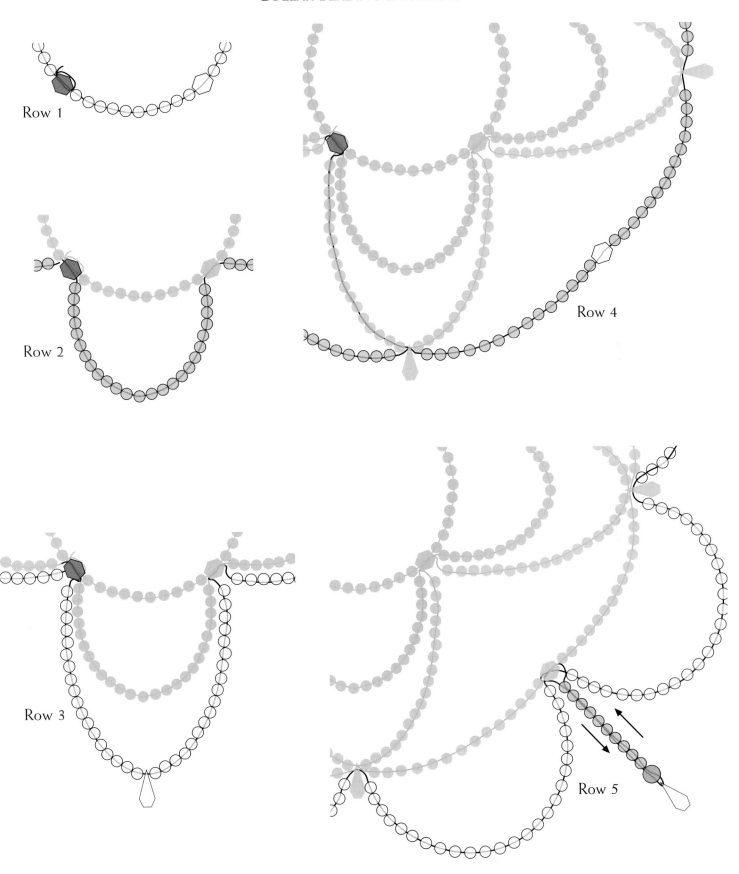

Row 1

Row 2

Row 3

Row 4

Row 5

IT'S A WONDERFUL LIFE

FLOCKED AND MATTE RED GLASS BALLS
(shown on page 27)

You will need 3" dia. red glass ball ornaments with metal end caps, matte spray sealer, fabric glue, 1/4"w brown checked and brown satin ribbons, tracing paper, white Saral® transfer paper, paintbrush, and a flocking kit (our kit includes flocking adhesive and assorted colors of flocking fibers).

Use spray sealer in a well-ventilated area and allow to dry after each application.

Matte Balls
1. Remove the end cap from each ornament. Apply two to three light coats of sealer to the ornament.
2. Carefully replace the end cap. Glue checked ribbon around the end cap. Knot satin ribbon through the hanger.

Flocked Balls
1. For each ball ornament, trace the pattern, page 165, onto tracing paper. Transfer the pattern to the ball. Repeat to draw swirls around the ball.
2. Working on one swirl at a time and following manufacturer's instructions, flock the swirls.
3. Paint a ring of flocking adhesive above and below the swirls on the ornament. Flock the rings.
4. Glue checked ribbon around the ornament end cap. Knot satin ribbon through the hanger.

FRAMED ORNAMENTS
(shown on page 27)

For each ornament, you will need a vintage Christmas card, craft glue, acrylic refrigerator photo frame, cardstock, scrapbook paper (optional), 1/4"w silver foil tape, brown satin ribbon, and assorted embellishments (we used brown checked ribbon, charms, tags, a jingle bell, and a brad).

1. Cut a saying and images, including a background image, from the card.
2. Trim the background image to fit inside the frame, glue it to cardstock, and add scrapbook paper photo corners, if desired. Glue the saying and remaining images to the background image. Insert the background image in the frame.
3. Remove the paper backing and wrap the foil tape around the edges of the frame.
4. For the hanger, cut two 6" lengths of brown ribbon. Glue one end of each length to the back of the frame and knot the loose ends together.
5. Embellish the frame as desired.

GLITTERED GARLAND
(shown on page 26)

You will need transfer paper, illustration board, spray adhesive, silver glitter, fabric glue, and 3/8"w red ribbon.

Use spray adhesive in a well-ventilated area.

1. Using the desired font and point size (we used Garamond Bold font at 250 pts.), print "CELEBRATE THE SEASON" from a computer.
2. Transfer the outline of each letter onto the illustration board. Cut out the letters.
3. Spray the front of each letter with adhesive; apply glitter, allow to dry, and shake off the excess.
4. Glue 1/4" of one end of a 1 1/2" ribbon length to the top back of each letter for the tab (some letters may need more than one tab).
5. Wrap ribbon around the tree for the garland. Spacing the letters evenly along the garland, fold and glue the ribbon tabs over the garland.

GLITTERED SWAG
(shown on page 24)

You will need floral wire, wire cutters, artificial greenery and berry picks, glitter picks, small and large glitter snowflake ornaments, hot glue gun, red glass ornaments, matte spray sealer, transfer paper, illustration board, spray adhesive, silver glitter, fabric glue, and 3/8"w red ribbon.

Use fabric glue for all gluing unless otherwise indicated. Use spray adhesive and sealer in a well-ventilated area and allow sealer to dry after each application.

1. Wire the greenery picks together to form the swag.
2. Wire the berry and glitter picks to the swag as desired.
3. Wire the snowflakes to the swag and hot glue in place if necessary.

4. Remove the end caps; then, apply two to three light coats of sealer to the ornaments. Replace the end caps and wire the ornaments to the swag.

5. Follow Steps 1–4 of Glittered Garland to make the letters. (We used Garamond Bold font at 600 pts. for "CELEBRATE" and at 400 pts. for "THE SEASON.")

6. Hang the swag. Drape and attach two ribbon lengths below the swag. Spacing the letters evenly along the ribbon, fold and glue the tabs at the tops of the letters over the ribbon.

CREWEL PILLOW

(shown on page 25)

You will need $3/4$ yd of 45"w brown fabric, $1/3$ yd of 45"w red velvet, tissue paper, iron-on transfer pen, $1/4$"w brown checked ribbon, clear nylon thread, light green and beige fine sport weight yarn, beading needle, red seed beads, two 1" dia. brown buttons, fabric glue, $3/8$"w red velvet ribbon, and an 18" x 22" pillow form.

Use a $1/2$" seam allowance for all sewing.

1. Cut two 19" x 23" brown fabric pieces for the pillow cover. Cut a 10" velvet square; cut the square in half diagonally to form two triangles.

2. Trace the pattern, page 165, onto tissue paper. Turn the paper over and use the transfer pen to trace over the drawn lines on the back of the paper. Center the pattern, inked-side down, on the pillow front. Iron the image onto the pillow front.

3. Refer to the Stitching Diagram and pin checked ribbon lengths over the ribbon lines. Use clear nylon thread to machine stitch along the center of the ribbons. Refer to *Embroidery*, page 185, and embroider the design on the pillow front.

Stitching Diagram

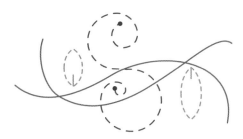

KEY
— Ribbon
--- Light Green Stem Stitch
— Light Green Straight Stitch
••• Beige Stem Stitch
• Beige French Knot

4. Adding seed beads to the thread as you sew, sew the buttons to the pillow front.

5. Pin the velvet triangles on opposite corners of the pillow front; topstitch along the edges. Glue velvet ribbon lengths to the pillow front, covering the diagonal edges of the triangles. Matching right sides and raw edges and leaving an opening to insert the pillow form, sew the pillow front and back together. Trim the corners and turn the pillow right side out. Insert the pillow form and sew the opening closed.

CREWEL CROPPED STOCKINGS

(shown on page 25)

For each stocking, you will need $3/8$ yd of 45"w red velvet, $3/8$ yd of 45"w brown fabric, tissue paper, iron-on transfer pen, $1/4$"w brown checked ribbon, clear nylon thread, light green and beige fine sport weight yarn, beading needle, red seed beads, two 1" dia. brown buttons, fabric glue, brown rickrack, and $3/8$"w red velvet ribbon.

Match right sides and raw edges and use a $1/2$" seam allowance for all sewing unless otherwise indicated.

1. Cut two $11 1/2$" x $12 1/2$" velvet pieces for the stocking front and back. Cut an 11" x 22" brown fabric piece for the stocking cuff.

2. Sew the stocking front and back together along one end and both long edges.

3. To create a boxed bottom in the stocking, refer to Fig. 1 and match one side seam to the bottom seam; sew across the corner. Repeat with the remaining side seam.

Fig. 1

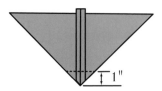

4. Sew the short ends of the cuff together. Matching wrong sides and raw edges and with the seam on one side, press the cuff in half. Unfold the cuff.

continued on page 126

5. Follow Steps 2–4 of Crewel Pillow, page 125, to add the checked ribbon and buttons and to embroider the design on the center of the cuff front with the bottom of the design ¹/₂" above the fold. Refold the cuff along the pressed line.

6. Align the seam in the cuff with one side seam in the stocking and match the right side of the cuff to the wrong side of the stocking. Sew the cuff to the stocking. Turn the stocking right side out. Topstitch the cuff and stocking seam allowances to the stocking approximately ³/₁₆" away from seam; trim the seam allowances.

7. Fold the cuff down over the top of the stocking.

8. Glue rickrack and velvet ribbon along the bottom of the cuff. Tack the ends of a 6"-long velvet ribbon hanger inside the stocking.

CREWEL TREE SKIRT
(shown on page 26)

You will need 1 ¹/₃ yds of 45"w brown fabric, pencil, thumbtack, string, ³/₈"w red velvet ribbon, 1 ³/₈"w red satin ribbon, tissue paper, iron-on transfer pen, ¹/₄"w brown checked ribbon, clear nylon thread, light green and beige fine sport weight yarn, beading needle, red seed beads, and 1" dia. brown buttons.

1. Cut a 45" square of brown fabric. Follow *Cutting a Fabric Circle*, page 186, use a 22" string measurement, and mark the outer cutting line for the tree skirt. Reinsert the thumbtack through the string 1" from the pencil and mark a second, inner cutting line.

2. Cut out the tree skirt along the drawn lines through all fabric layers. For the opening in the back of the skirt, cut through one layer along one fold from the outer to the inner edge. Unfold the skirt.

3. Clipping as needed, press the outer edge of the tree skirt ¹/₄" to the wrong side.

4. Sandwiching the pressed edge between the ribbons, pin a velvet ribbon length along the front and a satin ribbon length along the back outer edge of the tree skirt. Topstitch along the edges of the velvet ribbon to secure.

5. Repeating the design as desired and with the bottom of the design 2¹/₂" above the velvet ribbon on the tree skirt, follow Steps 2–4 of Crewel Pillow, page 125, to add the checked ribbon and buttons and to embroider the design.

6. Clipping as needed, press the remaining raw edges of the tree skirt ¹/₄" to the wrong side. Topstitch along the pressed edges.

TABLE SKIRT AND CREWEL TOPPER
(shown on page 28)

You will need a 30"h x 30" dia. round decorator table, 5¹/₃ yds of 60"w red velvet, pencil, thumbtack, string, 2¹/₂ yds of 45"w brown fabric, beading needle, red seed beads, clear nylon thread, 1" dia. brown buttons, ³/₈"w red velvet ribbon, tissue paper, iron-on transfer pen, ¹/₄"w brown checked ribbon, and light green and beige fine sport weight yarn.

Match right sides and raw edges and use a ¹/₂" seam allowance for all sewing unless otherwise indicated.

Table Skirt

1. Matching short ends, cut velvet in half along the fold. Cut one velvet piece in half lengthwise for the side pieces. Matching the direction of the nap, sew one side piece to each long edge of the center piece, ¹/₄" from the selvage.

2. Follow *Cutting a Fabric Circle*, page 186, use a 46" string measurement, and mark the cutting line for the table skirt. Cut out the table skirt along the drawn line through all the fabric layers. Unfold the table skirt.

3. Clipping as necessary, press the raw edges ¹/₂" to the wrong side; topstitch.

Crewel Topper

1. Cut a 32" brown fabric square. Follow *Cutting a Fabric Circle*, page 186, use a 15¹/₂" string measurement, and mark the cutting line for the topper. Cut out the topper along the drawn line through all the fabric layers. Unfold the topper.

2. Enlarge the pattern, page 165, to 133%. Use the pattern and cut twenty-two brown fabric pieces. Leaving the top edge open, sew two pieces together for a total of eleven points. Trim the seams and bottom corners; turn right side out and press.

3. Matching raw edges and overlapping the points to fit, sew the points to the topper.

4. Adding seed beads to the thread as you sew, sew a button to the end of each point.

5. Pin velvet ribbon along the topper seam. Topstitch along the ribbon edges.

6. Repeating the design as desired and with the bottom of the design 3¹/₂" above the velvet ribbon, follow Steps 2–4 of Crewel Pillow, page 125, to add checked ribbon and buttons and to embroider the design.

BUTTON PILLOW

(shown on page 25)

You will need ½ yd of 45"w brown fabric, thirty-six 1" dia. brown buttons, beading needle, clear nylon thread, red seed beads, and a 15" square pillow form.

Use a ½" seam allowance for all sewing.

1. Cut two 16" fabric squares for the pillow front and back.
2. Leaving room for seam allowances, spacing the buttons approximately 1" apart, and adding seed beads to the thread as you sew, sew six rows of six buttons to the pillow front.
3. Matching right sides and leaving one edge open to insert the pillow form, sew the pillow front and back together. Trim the corners.
4. Turn the pillow right side out, insert the pillow form, and sew the opening closed.

RIBBON PILLOW

(shown on page 29)

You will need ⅝ yd of 45"w red velvet, 14"l x 9" dia. neck roll pillow form or batting rolled into a cylinder, ⅝ yd of 45"w brown fabric, 5¼ yds of ⅞"w brown satin ribbon, 4½ yds of ¼"w brown velvet ribbon, and fabric glue.

Match right sides and raw edges and use a ½" seam allowance for all sewing unless otherwise noted.

1. Cut a 20½" x 29¼" velvet piece for the pillow cover and two 4½" circles for the pillow ends.
2. Matching short edges and beginning at each end, sew a 3"-long seam, leaving a large opening to insert the pillow form. Finger press the seam open.
3. Baste ¼" from each end of the pillow cover. Pull the basting threads to gather the pillow cover to fit the pillow ends, distributing the gathers evenly. Sew the pillow ends to the pillow cover. Clip the curves and turn right side out.
4. Insert the pillow form, fold the raw edges of the pillow cover ½" to the wrong side, and sew the opening closed.
5. Cut two 8¾" x 15¼" brown fabric pieces for the band and one 8¾" x 28½" piece for the lining.
6. For the woven ribbon area of the band, cut six 15¼" satin and five 15¼" velvet ribbon lengths. Beginning and ending ½" from the long edges of one band piece and matching the short ends, arrange the satin ribbon lengths ½" apart on the fabric. Glue the ends in place. Place the velvet lengths between the satin lengths and glue the ends in place.
7. Cut ten 8¾" satin and nine 8¾" velvet ribbon lengths. Beginning and ending 1" from the short edges of the fabric, weave the satin lengths, ½" apart, under the glued satin and over the glued velvet lengths. Glue the ends. Weave the velvet lengths over the glued satin and under the glued velvet lengths. Glue the ends.
8. Sew the band pieces together along the short ends; turn the band right side out. Sew the short ends of the lining together. Matching seams, place the band inside the lining. Leaving an opening for turning along one edge, sew the lining to the band along the raw edges. Turn the band right side out and sew the opening closed. Slip the band over the pillow.

FRAMED PIECES

(shown on page 29)

You will need wooden frames, brown acrylic paint, paintbrush, sandpaper, scrapbook papers, craft glue, assorted embellishments and tools (we used a vellum quote from a quote book, vellum tape, chalk, checked and striped ribbons, red embroidery floss, oval frame tag, adhesive foam dots, deckle-edged craft scissors, alphabet stickers, hole punch, brads, snowflake charm, pinking shears, round frame tag, oval cardboard tag, alphabet stamp set, black ink pad, and a "family" charm), vintage postcards, family photograph, and red velvet.

1. Remove the glass and backing from the frame and set the glass aside for another use. Paint the frame. When dry, lightly sand the raised areas for a vintage look.
2. Cut a scrapbook paper piece to fit the frame for the background. Place the background in the frame. Lightly mark along the inner edges of the frame with a pencil to define the usable design area. Remove the background from the frame.
3. Working inside the usable design area, glue embellishments to the background.
4. Mat or back the card or photo with scrapbook papers and velvet.
5. Use brads to attach embellishments and the image to the background. (The corners of our postcard image extend beyond the usable design area.)
6. Glue additional embellishments to the image.
7. Place the background and the frame backing in the frame.

LAYERED PACKAGES

(shown on page 27)

For each package, you will need a gift box; kraft paper and/or red wrapping paper; sandpaper; craft glue; floral, striped, or "handwritten" scrapbook paper; and assorted embellishments and tools (we used cream cardstock; brown chalk; 1/4" dia. eyelets, punch, and setter; brown rickrack; glitter snowflake ornament; brown and dark brown satin ribbons; brown checked ribbon; red velvet ribbon; metal alphabet charm; 4" x 6" index card; brown fabric scrap; tissue paper; iron-on transfer pen; light green fine sport weight yarn; beading needle; clear nylon thread; red seed beads; and a 1" dia. brown button).

Wrap each gift box in kraft paper or wrapping paper. Lightly sand the edges of the wrapping paper for a vintage look. Adjust embellishment sizes as needed to fit your package.

Package with Snowflake Tag
1. Glue a piece of torn floral paper to the package front.
2. Cut a rectangular tag from cardstock. Trim the corners from one end and chalk the edges. Set an eyelet on the trimmed end; then, tie rickrack through the eyelet for the hanger. Attach the snowflake ornament to the tag.
3. Tie brown ribbon around the package, catching the tag hanger in the knot.

Monogrammed Package
1. Layer and glue wrapping paper and torn striped paper on the package front.

2. Using the desired font and point size (we used Garamond Bold font at 600 pts.), print the desired letter from a computer and cut it out.
3. Draw around the letter on "handwritten" paper and cut it out. Glue the letter to the package.
4. Tie brown checked and velvet ribbons around the package. Glue the alphabet charm to the knot.

Package with Embroidered Tag
1. For the tag, cut the corners from one end of the index card. Draw around the card on a piece of floral paper; cut it out. Sew the pieces together along the edges.
2. Cut a fabric piece 1/2" smaller than the tag on all sides. Omitting the checked ribbon lengths, follow Steps 2–4 from Crewel Pillow, page 125, to embroider leaves onto the center of the fabric and to add the button and beads. Zigzag the fabric piece to the tag center.
3. Set an eyelet at the top of the tag; then, tie checked ribbon through the eyelet for the hanger.
4. Tie rickrack and satin ribbons around the package, catching the tag hanger in the knot.

HANGING BASKET ARRANGEMENT

(shown on page 25)

Refer to Rose Arrangement to arrange greenery, berry picks, roses, and glitter picks in a basket with a flat back. Form a hanger from floral wire and attach it to the back of the basket.

ROSE ARRANGEMENT

(shown on page 28)

Hot glue floral foam in a white container. Taping short-stemmed items to floral picks if needed, clip and arrange artificial greenery and berry picks and antique pink roses in the container. Add three sizes of red velvet roses, beginning with the shortest and ending with three long-stemmed roses at the top. Fill in with glitter picks as desired.

SNOW NEWS

FOOTED BOWL

(shown on page 35)

You will need a large plastic bowl; cooking spray; plastic wrap; newspaper; foam brush; matte decoupage glue; light ivory, red, and green acrylic paints; paintbrushes; 1 1/4" dia. ball knobs; and a hot glue gun.

Use one part paint to three parts water for all washes.

1. Coat the outside of the plastic bowl with cooking spray; then, cover it with plastic wrap.
2. Cut strips from newspaper (ours measure approximately 3/4" x 6").
3. To papier-mâché the bowl, brush glue on both sides of each strip. Overlapping the edges of the strips, cover the outside of the bowl. Apply three or four layers and allow to dry overnight.

4. Remove the bowl and plastic wrap from the papier-mâché bowl. Paint the bowl with a light ivory wash and allow to dry.

5. Use small newspaper strips and repeat Step 3 to papier-mâché the ball knobs. Paint the knobs with a red wash and allow to dry. Hot glue the knobs to the bottom of the bowl.

6. Roughly cut the rim of the bowl. Paint the edge with a green wash.

DOTTED BOWL
(shown on page 35)

You will need a medium plastic bowl; cooking spray; plastic wrap; newspaper; foam brush; matte decoupage glue; light ivory, red, and green acrylic paints; and paintbrushes.

Use one part paint to three parts water for all washes.

1. Follow Steps 1–4 of Footed Bowl to form the bowl and apply a light ivory wash.

2. Use red and green washes to paint large dots on the bowl; allow to dry.

3. Roughly cut the rim of the bowl. Paint the edge with a red wash.

PAPIER-MÂCHÉ PLATTER
(shown on page 35)

You will need a plastic platter, cooking spray, plastic wrap, newspaper, foam brush, matte decoupage glue, light ivory and red acrylic paints, paintbrushes, alphabet stamps, and a black ink pad.

Use one part paint to three parts water for all washes.

1. Follow Steps 1–4 of Footed Bowl to form the platter and apply a light ivory wash.

2. Paint two thin lines around the inner lip of the platter with a red wash and allow to dry.

3. Randomly stamp "Brrrr," "Chilly," and "Frosty" on the front of the platter.

NO-MELT SNOWBALLS
(shown on page 35)

For each snowball, glue one end of cotton cord or bulky weight yarn to a 2" or 4" foam ball. Wrap the ball until it is covered. Dab glue on the remaining end and tuck it under.

PAPIER-MÂCHÉ SNOWBALLS
(shown on page 32)

You will need 9" party balloons, newspaper, foam brush, matte decoupage glue, cream twill tape, masking tape, light ivory acrylic paint, paintbrush, modeling paste, palette knife, and fine multi-colored glitter.

1. For each ornament, inflate a balloon to the desired size; knot the end.

2. To papier-mâché the balloon, tear small pieces of newspaper. Brush glue on both sides of each piece. Overlapping the edges of the pieces and leaving a 2" circle around the knot uncovered, cover the balloon. Apply three layers and allow to dry overnight.

3. Make a small hole in the balloon near the knot. Carefully remove the balloon from the ornament.

4. For the hanger, fold an 8" length of twill tape in half and knot 1" from the ends. Tape the knot inside the ornament and tape the opening closed. Apply papier-mâché over the taped opening.

5. Paint the ornament with a light ivory wash using one part paint to three parts water; allow to dry.

6. Tint the modeling paste with light ivory. Apply the paste to the top of the ornament with the palette knife; then, sprinkle glitter over the wet paste.

TIN STAR ORNAMENTS
(shown on page 32)

You will need utility scissors; tin star ornaments; craft glue; newspaper; small tag; light ivory acrylic paint; paintbrush; 1/8" dia. silver eyelets, punch, and setter; alphabet stamps; brown ink pad; and cotton cord.

1. For each ornament, cut a slit from the bottom to the center of one star and from the top to the center of a second star. Slip the stars together.

2. Glue newspaper to the tag; cut it out. Paint the newspaper with a wash using one part paint to three parts water; allow to dry.

3. Attach an eyelet to the tag and stamp "Brrrr" on the front.

4. Knot a cord hanger through the eyelet and the hole in the star.

SNOWMAN ORNAMENTS
(shown on page 33)

You will need craft glue; newspaper; white cardstock; light ivory, red, and black acrylic paints; paintbrushes; tracing paper; silver ball chain; wire cutters; cream twill tape; alphabet stamps; brown ink pad; liquid fray preventative; and clear nylon thread.

1. For each ornament, glue newspaper to cardstock. Paint the newspaper with a light ivory wash using one part paint to three parts water; allow to dry.
2. Use the pattern, page 166, and cut a snowman from the covered cardstock.
3. Glue a length of chain along the edges of the snowman.
4. Mix one part light ivory paint and two parts red; use a dry brush to paint the cheeks. Use the handle end of a paintbrush to dot the eyes with black.
5. Cut a 9" length of twill tape. Stamp "Chilly" on one end of the tape. Trim the ends and apply fray preventative. Tie the tape around the snowman's neck.
6. Use a needle to make a hole near the top of the snowman's head. Knot a nylon thread hanger through the hole.

STAMPED SNOWFLAKE SPANGLES
(shown on page 33)

You will need craft glue, newspaper, white cardstock, light ivory and red acrylic paints, paintbrushes, alphabet stamps, 3" snowflake stamp, black ink pad, and cotton cord.

1. For each ornament, glue newspaper to cardstock. Paint the newspaper with a light ivory wash using one part paint to three parts water; allow to dry.
2. Cut two 2" dia. and two 3¹/₂" dia. circles from the covered cardstock.
3. Stamp the designs in the circles.
4. Mix one part water and two parts red paint; paint a border around the large circles.
5. Tie a 2" loop on one end of an 11" cord length. Sandwiching the cord ends below the knot between the circles, adhere the circles together in pairs.

GLITTERY SNOWFLAKES
(shown on pages 32–33)

You will need white cardstock, tracing paper, craft knife and cutting mat, craft glue, foam brush, fine crystal glitter, ¹/₁₆" hole punch, and twine.
For the newsprint snowflakes, you will also need newspaper, light ivory acrylic paint, and a paintbrush.

Cardstock Snowflakes

1. For each ornament, fold two 6" cardstock squares in half.
2. Use the pattern, page 166, and cut a snowflake from each folded square with the craft knife. Glue the folded centers together.
3. Brush thinned glue on each side of the snowflake. Sprinkle with glitter, allow to dry, and shake off the excess.
4. Punch a hole near the top of the snowflake. Thread twine through the hole and tie the ends together for the hanger.

Newsprint Snowflakes

1. Glue newspaper to the front and back of cardstock. Paint the newspaper with a wash using one part paint to three parts water; allow to dry.
2. Follow Cardstock Snowflakes and use the pattern on page 166 to complete each ornament.

SNOWFLAKE TREE TOPPER
(shown on page 32)

You will need a craft knife and cutting mat, ¹/₈"-thick foam core, foam brush, craft glue, fine crystal glitter, and white cardstock.

1. Enlarge the pattern, page 166, to 196%. Use the pattern and craft knife and cut one whole snowflake and two snowflake halves from foam core.
2. Brush thinned glue on each side of the snowflake pieces. Sprinkle with glitter, allow to dry, and shake off the excess.
3. Glue the halves to the center front and back of the whole snowflake.
4. Cut a 3" x 6" cardstock piece. Overlapping 1", glue the short ends together to form a tube. Glue the tube to the bottom back of the tree topper.

SNOWFLAKE GARLAND

(shown on page 32)

You will need tracing paper, 11" x 17" sheets of white paper (each sheet of paper will make a 60" length of garland), craft glue, mini snowflake punch, newspaper, and mica flakes.

1. Use the pattern, page 166, and trace four snowflakes along one short end of a sheet of paper. Accordion-fold the paper with the dotted ends of the patterns against the folds (Fig. 1).

Fig. 1

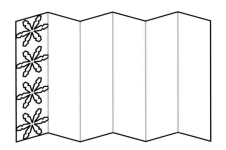

2. Cut the snowflakes out along the solid lines and unfold. Cut out and glue paper tabs to the back of the end snowflakes and glue the garland sections together to the desired length.

3. Glue mini snowflakes punched from newspaper to the centers of the garland snowflakes.

4. Dot glue on the points of each snowflake. Sprinkle with mica flakes, allow to dry, and shake off the excess.

STAMPED TWILL GARLAND

(shown on page 32)

You will need alphabet stamps, black ink pad, 1¼"w cream twill tape, silver brads, and ⅞"w silver snowflake charms.

Randomly stamp "Brrrr," "Chilly," and "Frosty" on twill tape. Use brads to attach snowflake charms between the words.

SNOW FELLOW

(shown on page 35)

You will need 6" and 9" party balloons for the head and body; newspaper; foam brush; matte decoupage glue; craft knife; masking tape; size 5 child's boots; two 3" dia. foam balls for legs; hot glue gun; tracing paper; white cardstock; craft glue; heavy-gauge wire; wire cutters; light ivory, orange, red, brown, and black acrylic paints; paintbrushes; two No-Melt Snowballs, page 129; cream bulky weight yarn; and a size H (5 mm) crochet hook.

Use decoupage glue for all gluing unless otherwise noted. Use one part paint to three parts water for all washes. Allow paint to dry after each application. Refer to Knit and Crochet, page 186, before beginning the project or use a purchased scarf.

1. Inflate the small balloon to 5" dia. and the large balloon to 8" dia.; knot the ends.

2. To papier-mâché the head and body, tear small pieces of newspaper. Brush glue on both sides of each piece. Overlapping the edges of the pieces and leaving a 2" circle around each knot uncovered, cover the balloons. Apply three layers and allow to dry overnight.

3. Make a small hole in each balloon near the knot. Carefully remove the balloons.

4. Use the craft knife to trim the hole in the top of the body to 4" or 4½" dia. so the head rests in the opening. Tape the head to the body. Apply papier-mâché to the head and body where they join.

5. Stuff the boots with crumpled newspaper. Place the foam balls in the boots and set the body on top, adjusting the boot placement as needed for a sturdy base. Hot glue the foam legs to the body. Set the boots aside. Apply papier-mâché to the legs and to the body where they join.

6. Use the pattern, page 167, and cut the nose from cardstock; clip the tabs on the curved end. Use craft glue to overlap and glue the straight edges together to form a cone; fold and glue the tabs to the head. Apply papier-mâché to the nose and head where they join.

7. For the arms, cut two 26" wire lengths and twist them together. Use the craft knife to cut two holes in the body. Thread the wire through the holes; bend the arms into the desired position. Wrap the arms with papier-mâché strips.

8. Use the pattern, page 167, follow *Making Patterns*, page 185, and cut two mittens from folded cardstock. Fold and use craft glue to glue a mitten over the ends of each arm. Wrap the mittens and "wrists" with papier-mâché strips, bending the mittens in a rounded shape to hold snowballs.

continued on page 132

9. Paint the snowman with a light ivory wash, the nose with an orange wash, the stripes on the mittens with a red wash, and the arms with a brown wash. Mix one part red paint to two parts light ivory; use a dry brush to paint the cheeks. Paint the mouth black. Use the handle end of a paintbrush to dot the eyes and buttons with black.

10. Hot glue a snowball to each mitten. Place the legs in the boots.

11. To crochet the scarf, chain 8. For Row 1, double crochet in the fourth chain from the hook and in each chain across: 6 double crochets. For Row 2, chain 3, turn; double crochet in the Back Loop Only, page 186, of the next double crochet and each double crochet across. Repeat Row 2 until the scarf measures 56" long; finish off. Refer to Fringe, page 186, to add 3"-long fringe to each end.

PAPER TREE ARRANGEMENT
(shown on page 35)

You will need red and green acrylic paints; paintbrushes; two sizes of matching square containers; floral foam; craft glue; three 5" x 7" magazines; $^5/_8$" dia. dowel rods; handsaw; hot glue gun; white spray paint; spray adhesive; crystal glitter; utility scissors; tin star ornaments; and paper shreds.

Use one part paint to three parts water for all washes. Allow paint to dry after each application. Use spray paint and adhesive in a well-ventilated area.

1. Use red and green washes to paint stripes around the containers.
2. Cut the foam to fit the containers and glue it in place.

3. For the small tree, working with three pages of one magazine at a time, refer to Figs. 1a–b to fold and make a 3" clip in the folded pages. Reposition the scissors and cut off the rest of the folded flap only as shown in Fig. 1c. Follow Fig. 1d to fold back the bottom section of the first three pages along the dashed line.

Fig. 1a   Fig. 1b

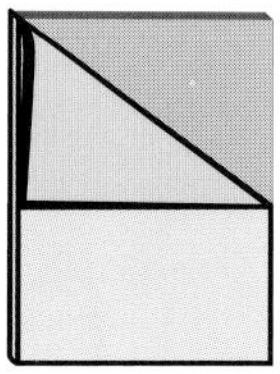

Fig. 1c 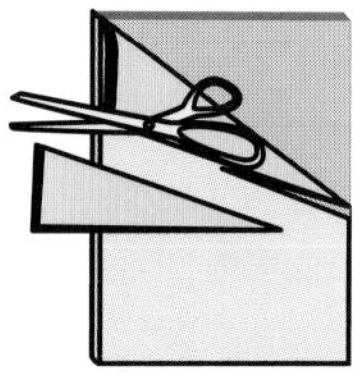   Fig. 1d

4. Continue to fold and cut all the pages of the magazine, varying the angle of the folds and cuts for added interest.
5. Matching the end of a 15" dowel rod length with the top of the magazine, hot glue the rod to the spine. Use craft glue to adhere the magazine covers together. Spot glue pages together as needed.
6. Lightly spray paint the tree; allow to dry. Spray the tree with adhesive and sprinkle with glitter. Allow to dry and shake off the excess.
7. Apply craft glue to the remaining dowel end and insert the dowel in the foam in the small container.
8. For the large tree, repeat Steps 3 and 4 to fold and cut the two remaining magazines. Stacking the magazines, follow Step 5 to hot glue a 22" dowel rod length to the spines. Apply spray paint, adhesive, and glitter and insert the dowel in the large container. Follow Step 1 from Tin Star

Ornaments, page 129, to make a dimensional tin star and hot glue the star to the top of the large tree.
9. Fill the containers with paper shreds.

FINGER CHAIN GARLAND
(shown on page 32)

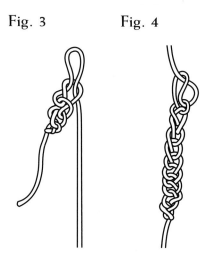

Make a slipknot near one end of a ball of chenille yarn, leaving a short tail (Fig. 1). Make a loop in the long yarn end and thread it partway through the first loop. Pull the tail to slightly tighten the knot (Fig. 2). Refer to Fig. 3 and continue threading a yarn loop through the previous loop until the chain reaches the desired length. To finish off a section, thread the long yarn end through the last loop and pull to tighten (Fig. 4).

Fig. 1   Fig. 2

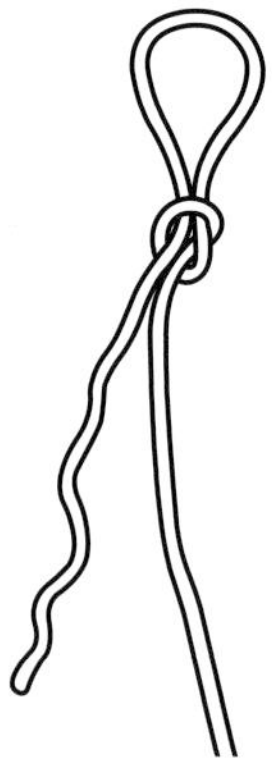

Fig. 3   Fig. 4

A Beach House Christmas

TAG ORNAMENTS

(shown on page 41)

You will need sandpaper, wooden tags, tack cloth, brown ink pad, Family and Inspirational Thinkable Inkables™, square eyelets, craft glue, brown chalk, green scrapbook paper, assorted embellishments (we used artificial eucalyptus, money plant leaves, and ming fern greenery; seashells; starfish; wire; metal sentiment tag; twill tape; and rub-on letters), cotton cord, and jute twine.

1. Sand the edges of each tag; wipe with the tack cloth. Lightly rub the ink pad on the edges and front of the tag.
2. Stamp words on the tag.
3. Dip an eyelet in glue; then, insert the eyelet into the hole in the tag.
4. Chalk the edges of a torn green paper rectangle; glue to the tag. Embellish the tag as desired.
5. Knot a 12" length of cord and twine through the eyelet for the hanger.

PAINTED JINGLE BELLS

(shown on page 43)

You will need blue, brown, and ivory acrylic paints; crackle medium; paintbrushes; jingle bells; matte spray sealer; ribbon; and jute twine.

Allow the paint and crackle medium to dry after each application. Use spray sealer in a well-ventilated area.

Basecoat each jingle bell with blue or brown paint. Apply the crackle medium; then, topcoat the bells with ivory. Apply sealer. Tie ribbon or twine hangers on the bells.

SHELL GARLAND

(shown on page 42)

You will need a hand drill with a 1/8" bit; seashells; 1/8" dia. hole punch; artificial money plant leaves; jute twine; jute rope; netting ribbon; Painted Jingle Bells; and starfish.

1. Drill a hole through each seashell. Punch a hole through each money plant leaf.
2. Cut a 4' length each of twine, rope, and netting ribbon.
3. Knotting each item in place as you go, string shells, bells, and leaves on the twine.
4. Randomly knot the rope to the twine. Tie the netting ribbon to the twine ends. Use twine to tie starfish to the netting ribbon.

STARFISH ORNAMENTS

(shown on page 42)

Thread a fishing line hanger through a 1/8" hand-drilled hole in one leg of each bleached starfish.

MESSAGE IN A BOTTLE

(shown on page 45)

You will need a pre-printed vellum sentiment, glass bottle with a cork stopper, sand, small seashells, brown and cream striped ribbon, cotton cord, jute twine, hot glue gun, and a small starfish.

Use small plastic bottles and add a jute hanger to make Message in a Bottle Ornaments, shown on page 42.

1. Tear the edges of the vellum sentiment. Roll up the vellum and insert it in the bottle.
2. Pour sand and shells into the bottle and add the stopper.
3. Tie ribbon, cord, and twine around the neck of the bottle. Hot glue a starfish and shell to the knot.

BASKETS OF GIFTS

(shown on page 40)

You will need gifts wrapped in kraft or handmade papers; craft glue; green scrapbook paper; ribbon, jute twine, cotton cord, netting ribbon, cream raffia, and natural bouclé yarn for ties; hot glue gun; assorted embellishments (we used seashells, sand dollars, starfish, and artificial eucalyptus and money plant leaves); alphabet stamps; brown ink pad; Tag Ornament; rub-on letters; small paper sacks; brown photo corners; 4" x 6" index cards; wooden tag; sandpaper; tack cloth; brown pencil; and baskets.

Use craft glue unless otherwise noted.

Gift Boxes

Glue torn paper squares or bands to the wrapped boxes. Add ties and hot glue embellishments to the boxes. For labels, write a message on the box, stamp a name on a sand dollar, or tie a Tag Ornament with a rub-on name to a ribbon.

continued on page 134

Gift Bags

Tie up a paper sack with ribbon, twine, and cord. Hot glue a shell to the bow. Or fold the top of a bag to the front and hot glue embellishments to the flap.

Gift Baskets

For each basket label, glue photo corners to an index card. Glue torn paper rectangles to the label. Follow Step 1 of Tag Ornaments, page 133, to prepare a wooden tag. Stamp and write on the tag; then, glue the tag to the label. Hot glue netting ribbon, shells, and a starfish to the tag. Hot glue the label to the basket.

TABLE RUNNER

(shown on page 39)

 You will need 2 yds each of 45"w linen-look fabric and embroidered sheer fabric, 2 yds bead and shell trim, clear nylon thread, and a beading needle.

Yardages will make a 14¹/₂" x 69" table runner; adjust yardages for other sizes. Use a ¹/₄" seam allowance for all sewing.

1. Cut two 15" x 70" pieces from linen-look fabric and one from sheer fabric, being careful not to cut through embroidered areas.
2. Cut two 14¹/₂" lengths of trim; set aside. Cut the beads and shells from the remaining trim. Sew bead-and-shell tassels to the embroidered motifs.
3. Layer the sheer piece right side up on a linen-look piece. Place the remaining linen-look piece wrong side up on the sheer piece. Sew together along the long edges, being careful not to catch any beads in the stitching. Turn the runner right side out.

4. Press the ends of the runner ¹/₂" to the inside. Sandwich the flange of a 14¹/₂" trim piece between the folds on each end; topstitch.

SHELL CANDLES

(shown on page 38)

 For each candle, you will need a clam shell half; thick towel; waxed, weighted wick; crème wax; and a glass container.

Never leave burning candles unattended.

Place the clam shell half on a thick towel for stability. Place the wick in the center of the shell half. Follow manufacturer's instructions to melt crème wax in the glass container in the microwave. Fill the shell half-full with the melted wax. Allow the wax to shrink and cool overnight. Fill the shell with more melted wax. Trim the wick to ¹/₄" from the wax.

GLASS CENTERPIECE

(shown on page 39)

 You will need a large glass compote; sand; netting ribbon; seashells; bleached starfish; river rocks; and artificial eucalyptus, money plant stems, and ming fern greenery.

1. Pour sand in the clean, dry compote. Place the ribbon in the compote, draping the ends over the sides.
2. Arrange the shells, starfish, and river rocks in the bowl. Fill in with the stems and greenery.

SERVING TRAY

(shown on page 45)

 You will need white, brown, and cream handmade papers; flat-bottomed basket with handles; clear acrylic sheet, cut to fit in basket; hole punch; jute twine; rub-on letters; craft glue; artificial eucalyptus, money plant leaves, and ming fern greenery; netting ribbon; ⁵/₈"w tan satin ribbon; hot glue gun; and a bleached starfish.

1. Tear the white paper to fit in the bottom of the basket.
2. Cut two brown paper tags. Punch a hole in each tag and tie a twine length through each hole.
3. Tear two cream paper rectangles to fit in the center of the tags; rub on "drinks" and "treats."
4. Use craft glue to glue the tags and several eucalyptus leaves to the torn paper. Randomly machine stitch over the tags and leaves. Place the stitched paper and acrylic sheet in the tray.
5. Tie the ribbon lengths around one handle, catching leaves and greenery in the knot. Hot glue the starfish to the knot.

TAG ADVENT CALENDAR

(shown on page 44)

 You will need a 16" x 20" unfinished wood frame with backing; foam core; craft glue; assorted handmade papers; blue and ivory acrylic paints; paintbrushes; crackle medium; matte spray sealer; netting ribbon; jute rope; staple gun; tracing

paper; pre-printed vellum holiday sentiments; patterned vellum (optional); assorted embellishments (we used a jingle bell; scrapbook papers; tissue paper numbers; number stickers; artificial eucalyptus, money plant leaves, and ming fern greenery; miniature sweater, hat, mitten, and clothespins; seashells; sea glass; starfish; keys; charms; metal sentiment tag; bead and shell trim; and a postmark sticker); hot glue gun; 1/4" dia. hole punch; cotton cord; jute twine; ribbon; T-pins; straight pins; and push-pins.

Use sealer in a well-ventilated area. Allow paint, crackle medium, and sealer to dry after each application.

1. Remove the backing from the frame and cut the foam core the same size as the backing. Glue a sheet of handmade paper to the foam core.
2. Refer to Painted Jingle Bells, page 133, to paint, crackle, and seal the frame and the jingle bell. Insert the covered foam core and the backing into the frame.
3. Cut two 20" lengths each of netting ribbon and jute rope. Staple one end of each length to the back of the frame. Knot the loose ends together at the top.
4. Use the pattern, page 167, and cut 24 tags each from assorted handmade papers and vellum sentiments. Place additional tags cut from patterned vellum over several paper tags, if desired.
5. Embellish the paper tags. Matching wrong sides, hold a paper and sentiment tag together; punch a hole through the layers. Tie the tags together with cord, twine, or ribbon.
6. Pin the tags to the covered foam core with the sentiments to the back. Turn one tag over each day to reveal a holiday message.

KNIT THROW
(shown on page 38)

Refer to Knit and Crochet, page 186, before beginning the project.

Finished Size: 38" x 46" (96.5 cm x 117 cm)

You will need 4 skeins of Bulky Weight Yarn [6 ounces, 185 yards (170 grams, 169 meters) per skein]; and a 29" (73.5 cm) circular knitting needle, size 11 (8 mm) **or** size needed for gauge.

Gauge:
In Stockinette Stitch,
14 sts = 5" (12.75 cm) and
14 rows = 4" (10 cm)

THROW
Cast on 106 sts.

Rows 1-10: Knit across.

Row 11 (Right side): K14, P2, K2, P2, (K12, P2, K2, P2) across to last 14 sts, K14.

Row 12: K3, P1, K8, ★ P2, (K2, P2) twice, K8; repeat from ★ across to last 4 sts, P1, K3.

Row 13: K4, P8, ★ K2, (P2, K2) twice, P8; repeat from ★ across to last 4 sts, K4.

Row 14: K3, P11, K2, P2, K2, (P12, K2, P2, K2) across to last 14 sts, P11, K3.

Rows 15-18: Repeat Rows 11-14.

Row 19: Knit across.

Row 20: K3, (P2, K2) twice, (P12, K2, P2, K2) across to last 5 sts, P2, K3.

Row 21: K5, P2, K2, P2, ★ K2, P8, (K2, P2) twice; repeat from ★ across to last 5 sts, K5.

Row 22: K3, P2, (K2, P2) twice, ★ K8, P2, (K2, P2) twice; repeat from ★ across to last 3 sts, K3.

Row 23: K5, P2, K2, P2, (K12, P2, K2, P2) across to last 5 sts, K5.

Rows 24-27: Repeat Rows 20-23.

Row 28: K3, purl across to last 3 sts, K3.

Repeat Rows 11-28 for pattern until Throw measures approximately 44" (112 cm) from cast on edge, ending by working Row 28.

Last 10 Rows: Knit across.

Bind off all sts.

KNIT PILLOW
(shown on page 38)

Refer to Knit and Crochet, page 186, before beginning the project.

Finished Size: 14" (35.5 cm) square

You will need 1 skein of Bulky Weight Yarn [6 ounces, 185 yards (170 grams, 169 meters) per skein]; 2 skeins of Bulky Weight Eyelash Novelty Yarn [1 3/4 ounces, 72 yards (50 grams, 66 meters) per skein]; straight knitting needles, size 17 (12.75 mm) **or** size needed for gauge; 14" (35.5 cm) pillow form; and a yarn needle.

Note: Pillow is worked holding one strand of each yarn together throughout.

continued on page 136

Gauge:
In Stockinette Stitch,
9 sts = 4¹/₂" (12 cm) and
12 rows = 4" (10 cm)

FRONT
Cast on 32 sts.

Row 1: Purl across.

Row 2 (Right side): K1, P2, K5, (P3, K5) across.

Row 3: P6, (K3, P5) across to last 2 sts, K1, P1.

Row 4: K6, (P3, K5) across to last 2 sts, P1, K1.

Row 5: P1, K2, P5, (K3, P5) across.

Row 6: K4, P3, (K5, P3) across to last st, K1.

Row 7: P2, K3, (P5, K3) across to last 3 sts, P3.

Row 8: K2, P3, (K5, P3) across to last 3 sts, K3.

Row 9: P4, K3, (P5, K3) across to last st, P1.

Rows 10-41: Repeat Rows 2-9, 4 times.

Row 42: Knit across.

Bind off all sts in **purl**.

BACK
Work same as Front.

ASSEMBLY
Matching **wrong** sides and leaving an opening for turning, sew the Front and Back together. Insert the pillow form and sew the opening closed.

EMBELLISHED PILLOW
(shown on page 38)

You will need ¹/₂ yd each of 45"w linen-look fabric and embroidered sheer fabric, 2 yds bead and shell trim, clear nylon thread, beading needle, and a 14" square pillow form.

Use a ¹/₂" seam allowance for all sewing.

1. Cut two 15" squares from linen-look fabric and one from sheer fabric, being careful not to cut through the embroidered areas.
2. For the pillow front, layer the sheer square right side up on top of one linen-look square. Pin and baste the trim along the edges.
3. Matching right sides and leaving one edge open for inserting the pillow form, sew the pillow front and back together. Trim the corners and turn right side out.
4. Cut the beads and shells from the remaining trim. Sew bead-and-shell tassels to the embroidered motifs on the pillow front.
5. Insert the pillow form and sew the opening closed.

SEASIDE SWAG
(shown on page 41)

You will need floral wire; wire cutters; artificial ming fern greenery, eucalyptus, and money plant stems; hot glue gun; sand dollar; starfish; seashells; and a cork star with a jute hanger.

1. Wire two fern branches end-to-end. Wire eucalyptus and money plant stems to the branches.
2. Hot glue the sand dollar, starfish, and shells to the garland.
3. Hot glue a money plant stem to the back of the cork star. Hang the star from the center of the garland.

WRAPPED CANDLE HOLDER
(shown on page 37)

You will need white and brown handmade paper, tracing paper, craft knife, cutting mat, craft glue, 7¹/₂"h x 3¹/₂" dia. clear glass candle holder, jute twine, cotton cord, one eucalyptus and two money plant artificial leaves, and small buttons or shells.

A short candle will glow through the cutouts. Never leave burning candles unattended.

1. Tear a 5¹/₂" x 12" white paper strip and a 4¹/₂" x 12" brown paper strip.
2. Use the pattern, page 167, and cut two stars from the center of the brown paper, 1¹/₂" apart. Glue the papers together.
3. Wrap and glue the papers around the candle holder.
4. Wrap the twine and cord twice around the candle holder and tie a tight knot around the stems of the leaves. Leaving the ends long, tie buttons or shells on the twine ends.

CASCADE
(shown on page 43)

You will need artificial ming fern greenery, eucalyptus, and money plant stems; floral wire; wire cutters; cork stars with jute hangers; blue and ivory Painted Jingle Bells, page 133; netting ribbon; hot glue gun; and a bleached starfish.

1. Hang the greenery and stems upside down and wire the ends together. Wire the stars and the bells to the cascade.
2. Tie a ribbon hanger with streamers around the top. Hot glue the starfish to the knot.

WIND CHIMES

(shown on page 42)

You will need a hand drill with a $^1/_8$" bit; seashells; one natural, one large, and one small bleached starfish; fine and medium jute twine; sand dollar; Painted Jingle Bells, page 133; and sea glass.

1. Drill a hole through each seashell and the center of each starfish. Drill a hole through the end of each arm of the large bleached starfish.
2. Hold one 30" fine twine length and three 30" medium twine lengths together and tie a 3" loop hanger on one end. Tying a knot below each item, thread the twine through the center of the natural starfish, the bleached starfish with the arm holes, and a shell. Tie the sand dollar to the twine. Add the remaining starfish and tie three bells at the bottom.
3. Knot a 20" fine twine length through each starfish arm hole. Knotting each item in place as you go, string shells, sea glass, and bells on the twine; trim the twine to different lengths.

WHIMSICAL CHRISTMAS

PAINTED CHRISTMAS TREES

(shown on page 47)

You will need a handsaw; two $^3/_8$" x 36" dowel rods; drill; three 5" dia. wood plaques; craft glue; red, ivory, green, and light green acrylic paints; paintbrushes; $1^1/_4$ yds of 60"w canvas; quick-drying fabric glue; glitter; rubber bands; hot glue gun; duct tape; medium-gauge wire; and wire cutters.

Allow paint to dry after each application. Apply additional coats as needed.

1. Cut one 19", 18", and 14" dowel length. Drill a $^3/_8$" dia. hole partly through the center of each plaque. Glue a dowel in each hole.
2. Paint the bases and dowels as shown.
3. Photocopy the pattern, page 174, at 100% to 250% in 25% increments, making seven patterns.
4. For the large tree, use the five largest patterns and cut the shapes from canvas.
5. For each of the two smaller trees, use the five smallest patterns and cut the shapes from canvas.
6. Fold the canvas shapes into cones and glue with fabric glue.
7. Alternate colors and paint the cones green and light green. Paint a second coat on each piece and paint the inside the same color as the outside. Run a bead of fabric glue along the bottom edges and sprinkle glitter on the glue. Allow to dry and shake off the excess.
8. Cut just enough of the tip from the bottom four cones so the cones will slide onto the dowel.

9. For each tree, wrap a rubber band on the dowel and slide the largest cone on the dowel. Adjusting the rubber bands as needed, repeat to place the next three cones on the dowel.
10. Hot glue the top cone to the top of the 18" dowel. For the bent trees, tape wire to the top of the remaining dowels. Hot glue the top cones to the top of the wires. Bend the tops as desired.

MANTEL PACKAGES

(shown on page 47)

You will need white foam core; craft knife and cutting mat; red, ivory, green, light green, and light yellow acrylic paints; paintbrushes; $^3/_8$"w ribbons; and duct tape.

Allow paint to dry after each application. Apply additional coats as needed.

1. Refer to the photo and draw a lopsided package and package stacks on foam core (ours stand $9^1/_2$" to $12^1/_2$" tall). Cut out the stacks with the craft knife.
2. Paint the packages as desired. Add dots, stripes, swirls, or scallops.
3. Arrange the ribbons on the stacks; tape the ends to the back. Make ribbon loops and tape the ends to the back for the bows.
4. For each stand, cut a $2^1/_2$" x 7" strip from foam core. Score each stand 1" from one end. Tape the scored end just above the center back of the stack.

WHIMSICAL SANTA

(shown on page 48)

You will need red, green, light green, ivory, coral, light yellow, and flesh acrylic paints; paintbrushes; 17½" x 23½" oval wood plaque; two 3¾" dia. x ¾"-thick wood plaques; one ⅜" x 36" and two ¾" x 36" dowel rods; Gorilla Glue®; clamps; drill; two 12" wooden rulers; hot glue gun; craft knife and cutting mat; 32" x 40" sheet of white foam core; black craft foam; 1¼"w belt buckle; 18" x 24" sheet of red corrugated plastic; 1" dia. foam brush; white opaque flakes texture gel; glitter; two black shank buttons with the shanks removed for eyes; heavy-duty needle; medium-gauge wire; wire cutters; double-sided foam tape; three 25mm jingle bells; craft glue; and ⅜"w ribbons.

Allow paint and glue to dry after each application. Apply additional coats as needed. Follow manufacturer's instructions and use Gorilla Glue® for all gluing unless otherwise indicated.

1. Refer to the photo to paint the plaques and the bottom 22" of the ¾" dowel rods.
2. Mark the centers of the plaques. Place the round plaques with edges touching at the center of the oval plaque; glue in place. Drill a ¾" dia. hole through the center of each round plaque and partway into the oval plaque.
3. Measure the distance between the centers of the two holes. Use this measurement to mark the placement for the holes in the center of each ruler. Drill the holes. Insert the painted ends of the dowels in the plaque holes for the legs.

4. Thread the top of the legs through the holes in the rulers. Hot glue the rulers in place at 13½" and 5" from the top of the legs.
5. Enlarge the patterns, pages 168–171, to the indicated percentages. Use the patterns and cut the shapes from foam core. Cut one mitten with gifts in reverse, omitting the top gift. Cut a 2" x 26½" wavy strip from foam core for the coat cuff. For the belt, cut a slightly curved 1¼" x 16" and 1¼" x 12" piece from craft foam. Round one end of the 12" piece and thread it through the belt buckle.
6. Refer to the Diagram to cut Santa's coat and hat from corrugated plastic.

Diagram

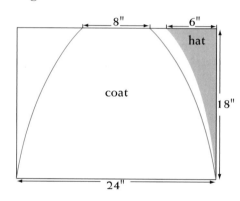

7. Refer to the photo to paint Santa's boots, face, nose, mittens, and gifts. Add details as shown, using the foam brush for the large dots. Paint the remaining dowel rod red.
8. Add texture gel to Santa's beard and mustache and while wet, sprinkle them with glitter. Allow to dry and shake off the excess.
9. Glue the mustache, eyes, and nose to the face, and glue the cuffs to the boots, coat, and hat. Wrapping the ends to the back, glue the belt to the coat.
10. Glue the boots to the legs. Center and glue the red dowel to the top front edge of the top ruler. Glue a mitten to each end of the dowel (Fig. 1).

Fig. 1

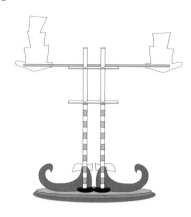

11. Center the coat 1½" below the top of the legs. Use the needle to punch holes 1" from the top edge of the coat; wire the coat to the legs. Tape the face to the coat and the hat to the face.
12. Punch holes through the tips of the boots and hat and wire the bells in place. For added stability, wire the hat bell to the package stack where it overlaps.
13. Use craft glue to glue the ribbons on the package stacks; make ribbon loops and glue the ends to the back for bows.

STAR TREE TOPPER

(shown on page 50)

You will need tracing paper, two 14" canvas squares; yellow, red, and green acrylic paints; paintbrushes; medium-gauge wire; wire cutters; batting; craft glue; and glitter.

Allow paint to dry after each application. Apply additional coats as needed.

1. Use the pattern, page 173, and cut a star from each canvas square.
2. Paint the stars yellow. Paint red spots; then, paint green circles around the spots.

3. Cut one 18" and two 9" wire lengths. Twist the wire lengths together to make a frame (Fig. 1).

Fig. 1

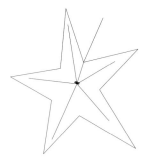

4. Wrap a 3" x 9" batting strip around the center of the frame. Place the frame on the wrong side of one star. Adjusting the wires and batting as needed and leaving a wire tail for a hanger, glue the star pieces together along the edges.
5. Working on one edge at a time, run a bead of glue along the edges and sprinkle glitter on the glue. Allow to dry and shake off the excess.
6. Bend the hanger into a coil.

STANDING PACKAGES
(shown on page 51)

You will need two 30" x 40" white foam core sheets; duct tape; craft knife and cutting mat; red, ivory, green, light green, and pale yellow acrylic paints; paintbrushes; and 1½"w ribbon.

1. Place the pieces of foam core end-to-end and tape them together along the back edges. Refer to the photo and draw a 52" tall lopsided package stack on the foam core. Cut out the stack with the craft knife.
2. Cut a 2½" x 15" foam core brace. Tape the brace to the back of the package stack over the taped seam.

3. Follow Steps 2–3 of Mantle Packages, page 137, to paint the packages and add the ribbon to the stack, being sure to cover the seam where the stack is pieced.
4. For the stand, cut a 4½" x 30" foam core strip. Score the stand 1½" from one end. Tape the scored end just above the center back of the stack. Use the craft knife to poke a hole 1" from the bottom of the stand. Tape one end of a 12" ribbon to the bottom back of the stack and thread the remaining end through the hole in the stand. Knot the loose end.

DOTTED SNOWY ORNAMENTS
(shown on page 50)

Use round foam brushes to paint dots on "snow-topped" glass ornaments. Add ribbon hangers to these simply unique tree decorations.

ORNAMENTS WITH KNIT COLLARS
(shown on page 50)

You will need glass ball ornaments with metal end caps, square and swirl punches, double-sided adhesive sheet, Soft Flock® fibers, silver leaf, dry paintbrush, red bulky weight yarn and size 9 (5.5 mm) knitting needles or purchased trim, and craft glue.

Knit or use purchased trim for the collars.

1. For each ornament, wipe the ball clean with a soft cloth.
2. Adhere squares punched from the adhesive sheet to the ball. Follow manufacturer's instructions and flock the squares.

3. Adhere swirls punched from the adhesive sheet to the ball. Apply silver leaf to the swirls and brush the excess from the ball .
4. For each collar, cast on 20 stitches and knit three rows, or cut a 6" length of purchased trim. Glue the collar to the ornament.
5. For the hanger, thread a length of yarn or trim through the end cap and knot the ends together.

PAINTED CANVAS ORNAMENTS
(shown on page 50)

You will need tracing paper; canvas sheets; ivory, red, and green acrylic paints; blending medium; paintbrushes; transfer paper; craft glue; and silver glitter.

Mix one drop of blending medium with each nickel-sized drop of paint. Allow paint to dry after each application. Apply additional coats as needed.

1. For each ornament, use the pattern, page 168, and cut four shapes from a canvas sheet. Paint both sides of each shape ivory. Transfer the detail lines onto the shapes.
2. For each shape, paint red stripes on the right half. Turn the shape over and paint red stripes on the left half.
3. Alternating with the red stripes, paint green stripes on the remaining sides of each shape.
4. Stack the shapes, beginning with the green stripes on the left side of the bottom shape and alternating colors on the remaining shapes.
5. Machine stitch the canvas layers together along the center line from the bottom to the top, leaving the top threads long and tying the ends together for the hanger.

continued on page 140

6. Separate the canvas layers. Working on one edge at a time, run a bead of glue along the edges and sprinkle glitter on the glue. Allow to dry and shake off the excess.

SKINNY DOTTED KNIT STOCKING
(shown on page 49)

Refer to Knit and Crochet, page 186, before beginning the project.

■■■□ INTERMEDIATE

Finished Size:
7¹/₂"w x 31"l
(19 cm x 78.5 cm)

You will need 1 skein of Red Bulky Weight Yarn [5 ounces, 255 yards (140 grams, 232 meters) per skein]; 1 skein of White Bulky Weight Brushed Acrylic Yarn [3¹/₂ ounces, 142 yards (100 grams, 129 meters) per skein]; straight knitting needles, size 9 (5.5 mm) **or** size needed for gauge; 3 stitch holders; and a yarn needle.

Gauge:
In Stockinette Stitch,
15 sts and
24 rows = 4¹/₂" (11.5 cm)

LEG
With Red, cast on 28 sts.

Beginning with a **purl** row, work in Stockinette Stitch until Leg measures approximately 24¹/₂" (62 cm) from cast on edge, ending by working a **purl** row.

Cut yarn.

LEFT HEEL
Note: When instructed to slip a stitch, always slip as if to **purl**, unless otherwise instructed.

Row 1: Slip 9 sts onto st holder (Right Heel), slip next 10 sts onto second st holder (Top of Foot), slip 1, with White knit across: 9 sts.

Row 2: Purl across.

Row 3: Slip 1, knit across.

Rows 4-13: Repeat Rows 2 and 3, 5 times.

Heel Turning: P1, P2 tog *(Fig. 2, page 186)*, P1, **turn**; slip 1, K2, **turn**; P2, P2 tog, P1, **turn**; slip 1, K3, **turn**; P3, P2 tog, P1, **turn**; slip 1, K4, **turn**; P4, P2 tog; cut yarn: 5 sts.

Slip remaining sts onto st holder.

RIGHT HEEL
With **right** side facing, slip 9 sts from Right Heel st holder onto empty needle.

Row 1: With White, knit across.

Row 2: Slip 1, purl across.

Row 3: Knit across.
Rows 4-12: Repeat Rows 2 and 3, 4 times; then, repeat Row 2 once **more**.

Heel Turning: K1, K2 tog *(Fig. 1, page 186)*, K1, **turn**; slip 1, P2, **turn**; K2, K2 tog, K1, **turn**; slip 1, P3, **turn**; K3, K2 tog, K1, **turn**; slip 1, P4, **turn**; K4, K2 tog; cut yarn: 5 sts.

GUSSET AND INSTEP
Row 1: With **right** side facing, slip 5 sts on right needle onto empty needle, with Red, K5, pick up 8 sts along side of Right Heel *(Fig. 6, page 187)*, slip 10 sts from Top of Foot st holder onto an empty needle and knit across, pick up 8 sts along side of Left Heel, knit 5 sts from Left Heel st holder: 36 sts.

Row 2: Purl across.

Row 3: K8, K2 tog, K16, slip 1 as if to **knit**, K1, PSSO *(Figs. 4a–b, page 187)*, K8: 34 sts.

Row 4: Purl across.

Row 5: K7, K2 tog, K16, slip 1 as if to **knit**, K1, PSSO, K7: 32 sts.

Row 6: Purl across.

Row 7: K6, K2 tog, K16, slip 1 as if to **knit**, K1, PSSO, K6: 30 sts.

Row 8: Purl across.

Row 9: K5, K2 tog, K 16, slip 1 as if to **knit**, K1, PSSO, K5: 28 sts.

Row 10: Purl across.

Row 11: Knit across.

Row 12: Purl across.

Rows 13-30: Repeat Rows 11 and 12, 9 times.

Cut yarn.

TOE SHAPING
Row 1: With White, K4, K2 tog, K1, place marker, K1, slip 1 as if to **knit**, K1, PSSO, K8, K2 tog, K1, place marker, K1, slip 1 as if to **knit**, K1, PSSO, K4: 24 sts.

Row 2: Purl across.

Row 3: ★ Knit across to within 3 sts of marker, K2 tog, K2, slip 1 as if to **knit**, K1, PSSO; repeat from ★ once **more**, knit across: 20 sts.

Row 4: Purl across.

Rows 5-8: Repeat Rows 3 and 4 twice: 12 sts.

Cut yarn, leaving a long end for sewing. Thread yarn needle with long end, weave needle through remaining sts, gathering tightly, and secure end.

BOBBLE (Make 40)
With White and leaving a long end for sewing, make a slip knot and place on needle: one st.

Row 1 (Right side): (K, P, K) in same st: 3 sts.

Row 2: Increase (see Increases, page 186), P1, increase: 5 sts.

Row 3: Knit across.

Row 4: P2 tog, P1, P2 tog: 3 sts.

Row 5: Slip 1, K2 tog, PSSO (Figs. 5a–b, page 187): one st.

Cut yarn and pull end through st.

Using photo, page 140, as a guide for placement, sew 20 Bobbles to each side of Stocking.

FINISHING
With **right** sides together and beginning at Toe, sew seam. Roll top of Leg over 1" (2.5 cm) to **right** side.

Hanging Loop: Holding 2 strands of Red together, cast on 12 sts.

Bind off all sts in **knit**.

Sew to seam inside top of Leg.

SKINNY STRIPED KNIT STOCKING

(shown on page 49)

Refer to Knit and Crochet, page 186, before beginning the project.

◼◼◼◻ INTERMEDIATE

Finished Size:
7¹/₂"w x 31"l
(19 cm x 78.5 cm)

You will need 1 skein of Green Bulky Weight Yarn [5 ounces, 153 yards (140 grams, 140 meters) per skein]; 1 skein of Green Bulky Weight Brushed Acrylic Yarn [3 ounces, 135 yards (85 grams, 123.5 meters) per skein]; 1 skein of White Bulky Weight Brushed Acrylic Yarn [3¹/₂ ounces, 142 yards (100 grams, 129 meters) per skein]; straight knitting needles, size 13 (9 mm) **or** size needed for gauge; 3 stitch holders; and a yarn needle.

Gauge:
In Stockinette Stitch,
15 sts and
20 rows = 4¹/₂" (11.5 cm)

LEG
With Green Bulky Weight Yarn, cast on 28 sts.

Row 1: Purl across.

Row 2: Knit across.

Rows 3-16: Repeat Rows 1 and 2, 7 times.

Cut yarn.

Row 17: With White, purl across; cut yarn.

Row 18: With Green Bulky Weight Yarn, knit across.

Row 19: Purl across.

Row 20: Knit across.

Rows 21 and 22: Repeat Rows 19 and 20.

Cut yarn.

Row 23: With White, purl across; cut yarn.

Rows 24-107: Repeat Rows 18-23, 14 times.

Row 108: With Green Bulky Weight Yarn, knit across.

Row 109: Purl across.

Cut yarn.

LEFT HEEL
Note: When instructed to slip a stitch, always slip as if to **purl**, unless otherwise instructed.

Row 1: Slip 9 sts onto st holder (Right Heel), slip next 10 sts onto second st holder (Top of Foot), slip 1, with Green Bulky Weight Brushed Acrylic Yarn knit across: 9 sts.

Row 2: Purl across.

Row 3: Slip 1, knit across.

Rows 4-13: Repeat Rows 2 and 3, 5 times.

Heel Turning: P1, P2 tog (Fig. 2, page 186), P1, **turn**; slip 1, K2, **turn**; P2, P2 tog, P1, **turn**; slip 1, K3, **turn**; P3, P2 tog, P1, **turn**; slip 1, K4, **turn**; P4, P2 tog; cut yarn: 5 sts.

Slip remaining sts onto st holder.

continued on page 142

RIGHT HEEL

With **right** side facing, slip 9 sts from Right Heel st holder onto empty needle.

Row 1: With Green Bulky Weight Brushed Acrylic Yarn, knit across.

Row 2: Slip 1, purl across.

Row 3: Knit across.

Rows 4-12: Repeat Rows 2 and 3, 4 times; then, repeat Row 2 once **more**.

Heel Turning: K1, K2 tog (*Fig. 1, page 186*), K1, **turn**; slip 1, P2, **turn**; K2, K2 tog, K1, **turn**; slip 1, P3, **turn**; K3, K2 tog, K1, **turn**; slip 1, P4, **turn**; K4, K2 tog: 5 sts.

GUSSET AND INSTEP

Row 1: With **right** side facing, slip 5 sts from right needle onto empty needle, with Green Bulky Weight Yarn, K5, pick up 8 sts along side of Right Heel (*Fig. 6, page 187*), slip 10 sts from Top of Foot st holder onto an empty needle and knit across, pick up 8 sts along side of Left Heel, knit 5 sts from Left Heel st holder; cut yarn: 36 sts.

Row 2: Purl across.

Row 3: K8, K2 tog, K16, slip 1 as if to **knit**, K1, PSSO (*Figs. 4a–b, page 187*), K8; cut yarn: 34 sts.

Row 4: With White, purl across.

Row 5: With Green Bulky Weight Yarn, K7, K2 tog, K16, slip 1 as if to **knit**, K1, PSSO, K7: 32 sts.

Row 6: Purl across.

Row 7: K6, K2 tog, K16, slip 1 as if to **knit**, K1, PSSO, K6: 30 sts.

Row 8: Purl across.

Row 9: K5, K2 tog, K 16, slip 1 as if to **knit**, K1, PSSO, K5; cut yarn: 28 sts.

Row 10: With White, purl across.

Row 11: With Green Bulky Weight Yarn, knit across.

Row 12: Purl across.

Row 13: Knit across.

Rows 14 and 15: Repeat Rows 12 and 13.

Cut yarn.

Rows 16-26: Repeat Rows 10-15 once; then, repeat Rows 10-14.

Cut yarn.

TOE SHAPING

Row 1: With Green Bulky Weight Brushed Acrylic Yarn, K4, K2 tog, K1, place marker, K1, slip 1 as if to **knit**, K1, PSSO, K8, K2 tog, K1, place marker, K1, slip 1 as if to **knit**, K1, PSSO, K4: 24 sts.

Row 2: Purl across.

Row 3: ★ Knit across to within 3 sts of marker, K2 tog, K2, slip 1 as if to **knit**, K1, PSSO; repeat from ★ once **more**, knit across: 20 sts.

Row 4: Purl across.

Rows 5-8: Repeat Rows 3 and 4 twice: 12 sts.

Cut yarn, leaving a long end for sewing. Thread yarn needle with long end, weave needle through remaining sts, gathering tightly, and secure end.

Finishing

With **right** sides together and beginning at Toe, sew seam. Roll top of Leg over 1" (2.5 cm) to **right** side.

Hanging Loop: Holding 2 strands of Green Bulky Weight Yarn together, cast on 12 sts.

Bind off all sts in **knit**.

Sew to seam inside top of Leg.

PAINTED TREE SKIRT
(shown on page 49)

You will need 1¼ yds of 60"w canvas; red, ivory, green, and light green acrylic paints; paintbrushes; tracing paper; transfer paper; and six 25mm jingle bells.

Allow paint to dry after each application. Apply additional coats as needed. Use a ¹/₄" seam allowance for all sewing.

1. Enlarge the section pattern, page 172, to 234%. Use the pattern and cut six sections from canvas.
2. Paint each section as desired. Paint 1"-wide stripes on two sections. Trace, then transfer the patterns, page 172, onto the remaining sections. Paint the designs.
3. Leaving two long edges unstitched, match right sides and sew the long edges of the sections together to form a skirt. Finger press the seam allowances open. Cut a circle from the center to fit around the tree.
4. Sew a bell to each point on the skirt.

BOTTLE CAP GARLAND
(shown on page 50)

You will need a glue stick; bottle caps with adhesive dots; circle, square, and swirl punches; patterned scrapbook papers; cardstock; and ⁵/₈"w ribbon.

Use the glue stick to cover the bottle caps with punched scrapbook paper circles. Add punched cardstock squares and swirls to the bottle caps as desired. Sandwiching the ribbon between the bottle caps, adhere the caps together in pairs.

ICY SPLENDOR

SILVER LEAF FRAMES
(shown on page 57)

In a well-ventilated area, spray black frames with metal leaf adhesive and place silver leaf sheets on the frames. Use a large, soft paintbrush to press the leaf into the adhesive; then, brush away the excess.

FRAMED ANGELS
(shown on pages 55 and 57)

You will need craft glue, silver scrapbook papers, Silver Leaf Frames with backing (we used 4" x 6" frames for the ornaments and 5" x 7" and 8" x 10" frames for the pictures), white vellum, vellum tape, silver glitter, mica flakes, faceted gemstones, and a 9" length of ¹/₄"w silver ribbon.

Ornaments

1. For each ornament, glue scrapbook paper to the frame backing.
2. Photocopy a star, if desired, and an angel pattern, page 175, onto vellum. Trim and tape the designs on the backing.
3. Spread thinned glue on the angel and adhere glitter and mica flakes to the design. Adhere glitter and a gemstone to the center of the star. Allow to dry and shake off the excess.
4. Insert the backing in the frame. Glue the ribbon ends to the frame back for the hanger.

Pictures

Photocopy a star, if desired, and an angel pattern, page 175, onto vellum at 127% for 5" x 7" frames and at 170% for 8" x 10" frames. Assemble the pictures the same as the ornaments, leaving off the ribbon hangers.

ETCHED ORNAMENTS
(shown on page 59)

You will need glass etching cream, round glass ornaments, craft glue, mica flakes, and silver glitter.

1. Follow manufacturer's instructions to etch the top third of each ornament.
2. Run a bead of glue along the edge of the etching and adhere mica flakes to the ornament. Allow to dry and shake off the excess.

3. Draw snowflakes on the ornament with glue and sprinkle with glitter. Allow to dry and shake off the excess.

EMBOSSED SNOWFLAKE ORNAMENTS
(shown on page 59)

You will need velvet (we used cream, white, and grey), cotton fabric for lining, 2" snowflake rubber stamp with wooden base, polyester fiberfill, clear nylon thread, beading needle, 1"-long silver bugle beads, clear silver-lined "E" beads, silver round beads, silver seed beads, 1¹/₂" leaf- and tear-shaped drop beads, and ¹/₄"w white sheer ribbon.

1. For each ornament, cut two 3" squares each from velvet and cotton fabrics.
2. To heat emboss the fabric, place the rubber stamp on an ironing board with the stamp side up. Center the velvet, right side down, over the stamp. Spray the velvet lightly with water. Press a hot iron on the wrong side of the velvet over the stamp for a few seconds; then, lift the iron. Continue pressing and lifting until the design appears on the back of the velvet.
3. Stack the velvet squares right sides together. Place the lining squares on top. Using a ¹/₄" seam allowance, sew all layers together along three sides. Trim the corners; turn the ornament right side out. Stuff and sew the opening closed.
4. Sew beads along the edges of the ornament. Add a drop bead to the bottom point.
5. For the hanger, sew the ends of a ribbon loop to the top back of the ornament.

EMBOSSED LEAF ORNAMENTS

(shown on page 59)

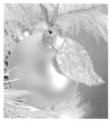

You will need a 2" leaf rubber stamp with wooden base, white and grey velvet, liquid fray preventative, craft glue, mica flakes, ball ornaments with metal end caps, and ¼"w white sheer ribbon.

1. For each ornament, follow Step 2 of Embossed Snowflake Ornaments, page 143, to heat emboss a leaf on velvet.
2. Cut out the leaf and apply fray preventative to the edges.
3. Glue mica flakes to the end cap and top of the ornament and along the edges of the leaf. Allow to dry and shake off the excess.
4. Glue the leaf to the ornament. Knot a ribbon hanger through the end cap.

BEAD GARLAND

(shown on page 59)

Thread assorted clear, smoky, and silver beads onto heavy-gauge wire. Use round-nose pliers to coil the wire ends to secure.

ICY WRAPPED PACKAGES

(shown on pages 56–57)

Adhere decorative papers to each gift box wrapped in white. Apply glue to the paper edges or to random spots on the package and sprinkle with mica flakes. Tie

sheer, satin, or glittered ribbon around the package; then, tie a Silver Leaf Frame, page 143, or tag enhanced with silver leaf to the bow. Or, tuck a crystal beaded-leaf spray or a clear acrylic ornament in a sparkly bow.

SNOWFLAKE TREE SKIRT

(shown on page 56)

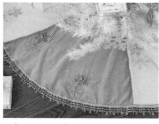

You will need kraft paper; 1¾ yds each of 45"w cream, white, and grey velvet; 2" snowflake rubber stamp with wooden base; metallic aluminum acrylic paint; paintbrush; 3" snowflake foam stamp; clear nylon thread; 5 yds of 1½"w sheer grey striped ribbon; 5 yds of 2"-long beaded trim; beading needle; assorted size bugle, faceted, seed, and "E" beads; and flat sequins.

Match right sides and long edges and use a ½" seam allowance for all sewing unless otherwise indicated.

1. Follow the Section Diagram to cut a pattern from kraft paper. Cut point from pattern as shown.

Section Diagram

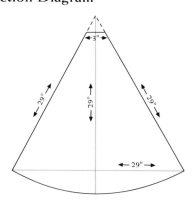

2. Use the pattern and cut two sections from each color of velvet.

3. Follow Step 2 of Embossed Snowflake Ornaments, page 143, to heat emboss snowflakes on each section.
4. Lightly brush paint over the foam stamp. Press the stamp beside each embossed snowflake. Remove the stamp and allow to dry.
5. Alternating colors, sew the sections together, leaving two long edges unsewn to create an open-ended skirt.
6. Matching wrong sides, fold along each seam and topstitch ¼" from the seam. Press the ends and top edge ¼" to the wrong side; topstitch.
7. Use nylon thread to zigzag the ribbon along the bottom edge of the tree skirt. Sew beaded trim to the ribbon.
8. Refer to the photo and sew a beaded and sequined snowflake beside each snowflake cluster and another on top of each paint-stamped snowflake.

SNOWFLAKE STOCKINGS

(shown on pages 54–55)

For each stocking, you will need a 22" velvet square (we used cream, white, and grey); ⅝ yd of 45"w white satin for lining and cuff; 2" snowflake rubber stamp with wooden base; 3" snowflake foam stamp; metallic aluminum acrylic paint; paintbrush; assorted size bugle, faceted, seed, and "E" beads; flat sequins; clear nylon thread; beading needle; 15" length of 2"-long beaded trim; and a 7" length of ⅝"w satin ribbon.

Match right sides and raw edges and use a ½" seam allowance for all sewing unless otherwise indicated.

1. Enlarge the pattern, page 174, to 209%. Cut front and back velvet stocking pieces (one in reverse) and front and back satin lining pieces (one in reverse). Cut a 7" x 15" satin cuff.

2. Refer to the photo and follow Step 2 of Embossed Snowflake Ornaments, page 143, to heat emboss snowflakes on the stocking front.

3. Follow Step 4 of Snowflake Tree Skirt to stamp a 3" snowflake on the stocking front; allow to dry.

4. Leaving the top edges open, sew the stocking pieces together. Clip the curves and turn right side out.

5. Refer to the photo and sew a beaded and sequined snowflake beside the snowflake cluster and another on top of the paint-stamped snowflake.

6. Sew the short ends of the cuff together. Matching wrong sides and raw edges, fold the cuff in half. Sew the beaded trim along the folded edge of the cuff.

7. Place the cuff over the stocking with the cuff seam in the back. Fold the ribbon in half for the hanger. Aligning the hanger with the heel-side seam, pin the hanger and cuff to the stocking.

8. Leaving the top edges open and an opening along one side for turning, sew the lining pieces together. Clip the curves; do not turn right side out.

9. Insert the stocking in the lining; sew along the top edges. Turn the stocking right side out; sew the opening in the lining closed.

EMBOSSED VELVET TABLE RUNNER
(shown on page 58)

You will need 2 yds of 45"w white velvet for the runner, 2 yds of 45"w white satin for the lining, 2" snowflake rubber stamp with wooden base, snowflake embellishments, silver-lined "E" beads, clear nylon thread, beading needle, 1 yd of 2"-long beaded trim, fabric glue, and 1 yd of ¹/₂"w white satin ribbon.

Match right sides and raw edges and use a ¹/₂" seam allowance for all sewing unless otherwise indicated.

1. Cut a 15" x 70" length each from velvet and satin.

2. Follow Step 2 of Embossed Snowflake Ornaments, page 143, to heat emboss snowflakes on the runner.

3. Sew snowflake embellishments and beads on the runner with nylon thread.

4. Sew the lining and runner together along the long edges only. Turn right side out.

5. Folding the raw edges under, sew beaded trim along each end. Wrapping the ends to the back, glue ribbon over the flange of the trim.

ETCHED CANDLE HOLDERS
(shown on page 58)

You will need glass etching cream, 9" and 14"-tall glass candle holders, craft glue, mica flakes, and silver glitter.

1. Leaving a 2"-wide band just above the center unetched, follow manufacturer's instructions to etch each candle holder.

2. Run a bead of glue along the edges of the etching and adhere mica flakes to the candle holder. Allow to dry and shake off the excess.

3. Draw snowflakes and dots on the candle holder with glue and sprinkle with glitter. Allow to dry and shake off the excess.

GLITTER & GLITZ

GLITTERED STARS
(shown on pages 62 and 64)

You will need tracing paper, glitter in assorted colors, sheets of poster board painted front and back to match glitter colors, stylus, spray adhesive, matching thread, and clear nylon thread.

For the Star Toppers, you will also need craft glue, heavy-gauge craft wire, and wire cutters.

Use spray adhesive in a well-ventilated area.

Glittered Star Ornaments

1. For each small ornament, use the pattern, page 178, and cut two stars from painted poster board. For each large ornament, enlarge the pattern to 129%, and cut two large stars from painted poster board.

2. Use the stylus to score the inner lines on each star. Refer to the pattern to fold along the red lines in one direction; unfold. Fold the blue lines the same way; unfold. Fold the grey lines in the opposite direction; unfold.

3. Spray the front of each star with adhesive; apply matching glitter and allow to dry. Repeat to glitter the back of the star and shake off the excess.

4. Staggering the points, use matching thread to tack the stars together at the center.

5. Thread a nylon thread hanger between the stars and around the thread; knot the ends together.

continued on page 146

Hanging Stars

For each hanging star, enlarge the pattern, page 178, to 343%. Follow Steps 1–4 of Glittered Star Ornaments, page 145, to assemble the star. For the hanger, cut two small slits through the top front point of the star (Fig. 1). Thread nylon thread through the slits to the back and knot the ends together.

Fig. 1

Glittered Star Toppers

1. For each star topper, enlarge the pattern, page 178, to 129% for a small topper or to 214% for a large topper. Use the enlarged pattern and cut two stars from painted poster board.
2. Follow Step 2 of Glittered Star Ornaments, page 145, to make fold lines on the stars. Cut a 1" x 2" rectangle from painted poster board. Glue the side and top edges of the rectangle just above the center back of one star to form an inverted pocket. Placing the pocket at the top back, follow Steps 3–4 of Glittered Star Ornaments to glitter and assemble the topper.
3. Spiral one end of a length of wire to fit around the top branch of the tree. Insert the other end in the pocket on the topper.

NEW YEAR ORNAMENTS
(shown on page 63)

For each ornament, using the desired font and point size (we used Antique Olive Black font at 250 pts.), print the desired year from a computer. Transfer the outlines of the numbers onto foam core and use a craft knife to cut them out. Sand the edges smooth. Working in a well-ventilated area, apply spray adhesive on one side and along the edges of each number. Sprinkle glitter onto a paper plate. Place the adhesive side of the numbers in the glitter and shake off the excess. Glitter the opposite side of the numbers. Center and glue the numbers on a 15" length of 2"w sheer metallic wire-edged ribbon. Notch the ribbon ends.

GLITTERED AND FLOCKED BALLS
(shown on page 63)

You will need glass ball ornaments, flocking kit (our kit includes flocking adhesive and assorted colors of flocking fibers), acrylic paints to match flocking fibers, paintbrushes, craft glue, and glitter.

For each ornament, paint four tilted rings around the ball using two different paint colors and allow to dry. Follow manufacturer's instructions and use a paintbrush to apply flocking adhesive and fibers on one ring at a time. Apply dots of glue around the center of the ball. Sprinkle the dots with glitter, allow to dry, and shake off the excess.

PARTY CRACKERS
(shown on page 66)

You will need orange and green cardstock, purple and turquoise foil origami paper, spray adhesive, orange and green glitter, craft glue, glitter ribbon, confetti, and turquoise and purple sequins.

Use spray adhesive in a well-ventilated area. Use craft glue unless otherwise indicated.

Orange Crackers
1. For each cracker, cut a 4½" x 5½" orange cardstock piece and a 5½" x 8½" purple foil paper piece.
2. Spray the front of the cardstock piece with adhesive; apply matching glitter, allow to dry, and shake off the excess. Spray the back with adhesive; center the foil paper on the cardstock. Roll the rectangle into a tube and glue the overlapping edges.
3. Tie a ribbon bow around one end of the foil paper. Fill the tube with confetti and tie the remaining end closed.
4. Glue turquoise sequins to the cracker.

Green Crackers

For each cracker, cut a 5" square from green cardstock and a 5" x 9" piece from turquoise foil paper. Follow Steps 2 and 3 of Orange Crackers; then, glue purple sequins to the cracker.

PARTY HATS
(shown on page 62)

You will need patterned scrapbook paper, craft glue, foil origami paper, and glitter.

1. For each hat, enlarge the pattern, page 176, to 120%. Use the enlarged pattern and cut a hat from scrapbook paper. Roll the hat into a cone, gluing the ends where they overlap. Clip the tip from the cone to make a $^3/_4$"w slit.
2. Cut a $1^1/_4$" x 18" foil paper strip. Cut 1"-long fringe along one long edge of the strip. Glue the opposite edge to the inner bottom edge of the cone.
3. For the topper, cut a $3^1/_2$" x 15" foil paper strip. Beginning at one end, accordion-fold the strip into twenty $^3/_4$" sections. To fringe the top, make 2" cuts along the folds. Insert and glue the uncut end in the top of the cone.
4. Apply dots of glue to the hat. Sprinkle the dots with glitter, allow to dry, and shake off the excess.

PHOTO CD PARTY FAVORS
(shown on page 66)

You will need turquoise satin, fabric glue, beaded trim, sequin trim, and sequins.

Use a $^1/_4$" seam allowance for all sewing.

1. For each favor, cut a $6^1/_2$" x $36^1/_2$" satin strip. Matching the right sides and short ends, fold the strip in half. Sew the long sides together, turn right side out. Finger press the raw edges $^1/_4$" to the wrong side; topstitch.
2. Fold the fabric 6" from the folded end to form a pocket. Topstitch along the sides of the pocket; turn the pocket right side out.
3. Fold the flap over and glue a length of beaded trim along the bottom edge of the flap. Glue sequin trim over the flange of the beaded trim, overlapping the ends on the back of the flap. Glue sequins to the front of the flap.

PARTY HORNS
(shown on page 66)

You will need craft glue; turquoise, orange, silver, and scalloped fuchsia sequin trims; fringed foil paper horns; double-sided tape; roll-out paper horns; glitter in assorted colors; tracing paper; and green scrapbook paper.

Alter and add embellishments to purchased party horns to coordinate with the other party decorations.

Fringed Horns
Glue sequin trims below the mouthpieces of Fringed Horns.

Roll-out Horns
Tape a spiral stripe on each Roll-out Horn, sprinkle with glitter, and complete with sequin trims.

Paper Tube Horns

For each Paper Tube Horn, remove the foil paper fringe from an extra horn. Use the pattern, page 176, and cut the shape from scrapbook paper. Roll the shape into a tube; glue the narrow end inside the mouthpiece and glue the edges where they overlap. Glue the scalloped trim inside the end of the tube. Apply dots of glue to the tube. Sprinkle the dots with glitter, allow to dry, and shake off the excess.

SPINNING ORNAMENTS
(shown on page 63)

You will need tracing paper; craft knife and cutting mat; mat board; poster board; spray adhesive; foil origami paper; pink, blue, and orange acrylic paints; paintbrushes; linen thread; craft glue; and medium silver sequins.

Use spray adhesive in a well-ventilated area.

1. For each ornament, use the patterns, page 179, and cut an ornament and a center each from mat board and poster board. Spray one side of each center piece with adhesive; apply foil paper and trim the edges. Choose a contrasting color and paint one side of each ornament piece; allow to dry.
2. Spray the back of each center and ornament piece with adhesive. Fold a 24" length of thread in half. Layer the pieces as shown, sandwiching the thread between the pieces with the loop at the top. Knot and trim the thread ends at the bottom.
3. Glue a row of sequins on the front and back of the center.

LARGE REVOLVING ORNAMENTS
(shown on page 64)

You will need tissue paper, transfer paper, foam core, craft knife with extra blades and cutting mat, sandpaper, glitter in assorted colors, acrylic paints to match glitter colors, paintbrushes, spray adhesive, craft glue, foil origami paper, 4mm silver beads, linen thread, and an upholstery needle.

Use spray adhesive in a well-ventilated area.

1. Enlarge the patterns, page 177, to 168%. Follow *Making Patterns*, page 185, to make a whole pattern on tissue paper. For each ornament, transfer the patterns to foam core. Changing the blade frequently to avoid tearing the foam, use the craft knife to cut out the ornament shapes. Sand the edges smooth.
2. Paint the front, back, and edges of the large and medium shapes and the edges only of the small shape; allow to dry.
3. Spray one side of the small shape with adhesive; apply foil paper and trim the edges. Repeat to apply foil paper to the opposite side.
4. Apply glue to the edges only of the large and small shapes. Apply matching glitter, allow to dry, and shake off the excess.
5. Spray one side and along the edges of the medium shape with adhesive; apply matching glitter and allow to dry. Repeat to glitter the opposite side and shake off the excess.

6. Without cutting the thread, string a bead on the thread and carefully feed the needle through the center top of the large shape. String a bead on the thread and take the needle around the bead and through the hole a second time to "lock" the bead just below the top of the large shape. Continue to feed the needle through the center top of the medium and small shapes and the center bottom of the small shape, adding another locked bead just below the bottom of the small shape. Feed the needle through the bottom of the medium shape. String a bead on the thread and knot the thread below this bead. Trim the thread end.
7. Determine the desired length of the hanger and tie a loop at the top of the remaining thread end. Trim the thread end.

SPARKLY CENTERPIECE
(shown on page 64)

You will need transfer paper, foam core, craft knife with extra blades and cutting mat, sandpaper, green and fuchsia acrylic paints, paintbrushes, four 18" x ³/₈" dia. dowel rods, spray adhesive, green and fuchsia glitter, Gorilla Glue®, clamps, floral gum, floral foam, aluminum bowl, kitty litter, metallic purple fabric, and ball ornaments.

Use spray adhesive in a well-ventilated area.

1. Using the desired font and point size (we used Antique Olive Black font at 700 pts.), print the desired year from a computer. Enlarge each number to 250%. Transfer the outlines of the numbers onto foam core. Changing the blade frequently to avoid tearing the foam, use the craft knife to cut out the numbers. Sand the edges smooth.
2. Paint the numbers and dowel rods as desired; allow to dry.
3. Spray the front and sides of the numbers with adhesive; apply matching glitter, allow to dry, and shake off the excess. Repeat to glitter all but the top 3½" of the dowel rods (glitter would prevent the rods from adhering to the numbers).
4. Follow manufacturer's instructions and use Gorilla Glue to glue the top of each dowel rod to the back of a number; allow to dry. Use floral gum to hold the foam in the bowl. Insert the dowels in the foam and pour kitty litter over the foam to stabilize the dowels. Arrange fabric in the bowl to cover the kitty litter. Place the ornaments in the bowl.

INVITATIONS
(shown on page 60)

You will need green and fuchsia cardstock, spray adhesive, assorted colors of glitter, tracing paper, poster board, foil origami paper, craft glue, beading thread, and pink and white rub-on letters.

Use spray adhesive in a well-ventilated area.

1. For each card, cut a 6" x 12" green cardstock strip. Matching short ends, fold the strip in half.
2. Spray the inside front half with adhesive. Fold the sprayed end to the center to adhere. Spray the outside folded front with adhesive; apply matching glitter, allow to dry, and shake off the excess.
3. Use the patterns, page 178, and cut two ornaments from poster board. Center one large piece over the outer fold of the card front. Draw around the half of the inside curve that falls on the card front; cut it out.
4. Apply spray adhesive to one side of each ornament piece; apply foil paper and trim the edges. Apply spray adhesive to the foil side of each medium piece and draw the year with craft glue on each small piece. Sprinkle the pieces with glitter, allow to dry, and shake off the excess.
5. Spray the back of each ornament piece with adhesive. Layer the pieces as shown, sandwiching a 5" length of thread vertically between the pieces. Trim the thread ends.
6. Matching the curved edges, glue half of the large ornament shape to the card front.
7. Apply rub-ons to the inside card front for the invitation message.
8. For each envelope, cut one 6³/₄" square and one 6³/₄" x 9³/₄" rectangle from fuchsia cardstock. Match the pieces on one end and glue the edges together along the end and two sides. Fold the flap over. Layer and glue strips cut from foil paper along the edge of the flap.

TABLE BANNERS
(shown on page 61)

You will need 4 yds each of turquoise satin for banners and cotton fabric for lining, fabric glue, 12 yds of silver sequin trim, 5 yds of fuchsia sequin trim, tracing paper, and transfer paper.

Our banners are designed to fit a 4'w table; adjust yardages as necessary to fit your table. Yardages are based on fabrics with a 40" usable width. Match the right sides and raw edges and use a ¹/₂" seam allowance for all sewing.

1. Cut three 19" x 67" pieces each from the banner and lining fabrics. Refer to the Diagram to trim one end of each piece to a point.

Diagram

9"

9¹/₂"

2. For each banner, sew one banner and lining piece together, leaving an opening in the straight end for turning. Turn the banner right side out; press. Topstitch ¹/₄" from all edges.
3. Glue a length of silver trim over the topstitching along the long and pointed edges of each banner.
4. Write "happy new year" on tracing paper and transfer one word to the pointed end of each banner. Glue the fuchsia trim over the transferred lines.

STRIPED CANDLES
(shown on page 67)

Never leave burning candles unattended.

Use a paper cutter to cut different-colored strips of varying widths from foil origami paper. Working in a well-ventilated area, apply spray adhesive to the wrong side of the strips. Overlapping at the back, wrap the strips around pillar candles.

CHARGERS
(shown on page 65)

For each charger, use a paper cutter to cut foil origami paper squares into ¹/₂"w strips. Working in a well-ventilated area, apply spray adhesive to the wrong side of the strips. Adhere the strips to the rim of an aluminum charger, with the strips touching along the inner edge of the rim; trim the excess. Use an adhesive strip applicator to reinforce strips as needed.

CHAMPAGNE FLUTE CHARMS
(shown on page 65)

For each charm, use rub-on letters to spell a name on flat oval beads. Alternating with seed beads or miracle beads, thread the oval beads to the center of a 6mm chenille glitter stem. Add a different colored bead on the top. Twist the beaded stem around the stem of a champagne flute.

NAPKINS

(shown on page 65)

For each napkin, cut a 10" square from lime fabric. Press the edges ¹/₄" to the wrong side twice; topstitch. Use fabric glue to glue ¹/₈"w turquoise, orange, or purple ribbon lengths over the seams, trimming the ends ¹/₄" beyond the edges of the napkin. Sew a sequin and a metallic seed bead at each ribbon intersection.

AMBROSIA PUNCH

Oranges can have varying shades of flesh. Pick two varieties (such as navels and red navels or blood oranges) to perch on the rim of your punch bowl for a contrasting garnish.

2¹/₂ quarts orange juice
2 cups pineapple juice
1 cup cream of coconut
2 small oranges, thinly sliced and halved
3 cups vanilla ice cream
3 cups ginger ale
¹/₂ cup flaked sweetened coconut, toasted (optional)

Combine first 3 ingredients in a punch bowl. Cut a slit halfway through each orange slice and perch slices around rim of punch bowl. Add tiny scoops of ice cream to punch bowl; add ginger ale. If desired, sprinkle some coconut over punch; serve remaining coconut in a small dish.
Yield: 4 quarts punch

CHAMPAGNE PUNCH

2¹/₂ cups orange juice, chilled
1 package (10 ounces) frozen strawberries, thawed and undrained
1 bottle (25.4 ounces) dry champagne, chilled

Process chilled orange juice and strawberries in a blender until smooth, stopping to scrape down sides; pour into a pitcher or punch bowl. Stir in champagne and serve immediately.
Yield: about 2 quarts punch

ROSEMARY PECANS

6 tablespoons butter, cut into pieces
3 tablespoons very finely minced fresh rosemary
¹/₂ teaspoon salt
¹/₈ teaspoon freshly ground black pepper
3 cups pecan halves

Combine first 4 ingredients in a foil-lined jellyroll pan. Bake at 400° until butter melts; remove from oven. Add pecans; toss to coat. Bake 6 to 9 minutes or until pecans are lightly toasted, stirring at 3-minute intervals. Let cool completely. Store in an airtight container up to 3 days.
Yield: 3 cups pecans

BLACK BEAN TARTLETS

(shown on page 61)

This Southwestern appetizer sports a red and green filling with spicy flavor.

1¹/₄ cups all-purpose flour
³/₄ cup yellow cornmeal
¹/₂ cup (2 ounces) shredded Monterey Jack cheese with peppers
1 teaspoon salt
1 teaspoon ground cumin
1 teaspoon chili powder
¹/₂ teaspoon garlic powder
¹/₂ teaspoon ground red pepper
¹/₂ cup cold butter, cut into pieces
1 large egg, lightly beaten
2 tablespoons ice water
Black Bean Salsa (recipe follows)
Garnishes: sour cream, fresh cilantro

Pulse process first 8 ingredients in a food processor until blended. Add butter; pulse until mixture is crumbly. Add egg and ice water; process just until the mixture forms a ball.

Divide dough in half; shape each half of dough into 16 (1-inch) balls. Press balls into lightly greased miniature (1³/₄-inch) muffin pans, pressing evenly into bottom and up sides.

Bake tartlet shells at 450° for 8 minutes or until lightly browned. Cool in pans 10 minutes; remove shells to wire racks and cool completely.

Spoon 1 tablespoon Black Bean Salsa into each tartlet shell; garnish, if desired. Serve at room temperature.
Yield: 32 appetizers

Black Bean Salsa

1 can (15 ounces) black beans, drained
2 canned chipotle chiles in adobo sauce, minced
3 green onions, chopped
1/2 cup finely chopped yellow bell pepper
1 plum tomato, finely chopped
2 tablespoons fresh lime juice
1 tablespoon chopped fresh cilantro
1 tablespoon olive oil
1/2 teaspoon salt

Combine all ingredients in a bowl, tossing well. Cover and chill at least 1 hour.
Yield: 2 1/4 cups salsa

Artichoke-Stuffed Mushrooms

(shown on page 61)

1 1/2 pounds large, fresh mushrooms
1/4 cup chopped onion
2 garlic cloves, minced
1 tablespoon olive oil
1/4 cup dry white wine
1/4 cup soft breadcrumbs
1 can (13.75 ounces) artichoke hearts, drained and chopped
3 green onions, chopped
1/2 cup grated Parmesan cheese
1/2 cup mayonnaise
1/4 teaspoon salt
1/4 teaspoon pepper
Garnish: pimiento pieces

Rinse and pat mushrooms dry. Remove stems and chop; reserve mushroom caps.

Sauté mushroom stems, onion, and garlic in hot oil in a large skillet over medium heat 5 minutes or until onion is tender.

Add wine and cook 2 minutes or until liquid evaporates. Stir in breadcrumbs. Remove from heat and let cool.

Combine mushroom mixture, artichokes, and next 5 ingredients. Spoon 1 teaspoonful of mixture into each mushroom cap. Place on a lightly greased rack in a roasting pan.

Bake at 350° for 12 to 15 minutes or until golden. Garnish, if desired. Serve immediately.
Yield: about 20 appetizers

Savory Cocktail Tree

(shown on page 61)

Rows of pimiento cheese balls, colossal olives, and wheat crackers create this one-stop hors d'oeuvre tree. All you need to enhance it is a glass of Chardonnay.

1 small onion, minced
1 garlic clove, minced
1 tablespoon butter or margarine
1/4 cup dry white wine
3 cups (12 ounces) finely shredded sharp Cheddar cheese
1 package (8 ounces) cream cheese
1 package (3 ounces) cream cheese
1 jar (4 ounces) diced pimiento, well drained
Coatings: 1 cup chopped fresh parsley, 3/4 cup finely chopped toasted pecans
1 12-inch-high plastic foam cone
2 tubs (8 ounces each) cream cheese, softened
1 1/4 cups chopped fresh parsley
1 package (10 ounces) baked bite-size whole-wheat snack crackers
2 jars (10 ounces each) large pimiento-stuffed olives, drained
1 large red bell pepper, cut in half lengthwise

Cook onion and garlic in butter in a medium skillet over medium-high heat, stirring constantly, until tender. Add wine. Bring to a boil; reduce heat and simmer, uncovered, until liquid has evaporated. Set aside.

Process Cheddar cheese and 11 ounces cream cheese in a food processor until cheeses form a ball, stopping once to scrape down sides. Remove mixture to a medium bowl. Stir in onion mixture and pimiento. Cover and chill at least 1 hour.

Shape mixture into 3/4-inch balls. Roll half of chilled balls in 1 cup parsley and half in 3/4 cup pecans. Cover and chill until firm.

Wrap plastic wrap around plastic foam cone, sealing completely. Spread softened tub cream cheese over plastic wrap-coated cone, covering cone completely and making a 1/2-inch thick layer. Sprinkle coated cone with 1 1/4 cups chopped parsley.

Press a circular row of crackers into the cream cheese-coated cone at the base. Attach a circular row of cheese balls at base of cone just above cracker layer, using wooden picks. Attach a circular row of olives above row of cheese balls, using wooden picks. Attach another row of cheese balls above row of olives. Gently press another row of crackers into the cream cheese-coated cone, creating a shingled effect. Repeat procedure, working in circular rows and covering cone completely.

Use a wooden pick to attach a parsley-coated cheese ball to top of tree. Cut a 1 1/4-wide star out of each pepper half, using a sharp knife or cookie cutter. Secure with wooden picks at top of tree. Serve any remaining cheese balls on crackers.
Yield: 6 dozen cheese balls

Mini Pork Sandwiches

 2 tablespoons chopped fresh
    rosemary
 1 1/2 tablespoons black peppercorns,
    crushed
 1 teaspoon salt
 3 pounds pork tenderloins
 2 tablespoons olive oil
 1/2 cup mayonnaise
 2 tablespoons prepared
    horseradish
 1 tablespoon brandy
 1 garlic clove, minced
 1/2 cup Dijon mustard
 3 tablespoons capers, chopped
    Several bunches arugula
    Sweet gherkin pickles, thinly
       sliced
 40 party rolls or small square
    dinner rolls

Combine rosemary, crushed peppercorns, and salt. Rub mixture over tenderloins. Fold thin end under each tenderloin; secure with wooden picks. Place tenderloins on a lightly greased rack in a broiler pan. Drizzle with olive oil. Bake at 375° for 25 to 30 minutes or until a meat thermometer inserted in thickest part registers 160° (medium). Let stand 5 minutes. Thinly slice tenderloins.

Combine mayonnaise and next 3 ingredients. Combine mustard and capers. Spoon sauces into separate serving bowls. Serve pork with sauces, arugula, gherkins, and rolls for making sandwiches.
Yield: 40 appetizers

Lemon Fondue

 2 jars (10 ounces each) lemon
    curd
 2/3 cup sweetened condensed milk
 1/2 cup half-and-half
    Strawberries, gingersnaps, and
       pound cake cubes to serve

Combine first 3 ingredients in a bowl and stir well. Spoon into a footed serving dish. Serve with strawberries, gingersnaps, and pound cake cubes.
Yield: 4 cups fondue

Cream Puffs with Chocolate-Mint Filling

(shown on page 61)

 1 1/3 cups water
 1 package (11 ounces) piecrust mix
 4 large eggs
    Chocolate-Mint Filling
       (recipe follows)

Bring 1 1/3 cups water to a boil in a medium saucepan; add piecrust mix and cook, stirring constantly, until mixture leaves sides of pan. Cook, stirring constantly, one additional minute. Remove from heat. Add eggs.

Beat dough at medium speed with an electric mixer for 2 minutes. Drop by teaspoonfuls onto ungreased baking sheets.

Bake at 425° for 20 minutes or until lightly browned and puffed; transfer to wire racks to cool. Make a horizontal slit about one-third of the way down from top of puff, cutting to, but not through, opposite side.

Spoon Chocolate-Mint Filling into a pastry bag fitted with a #21 star tip; pipe filling into each cream puff.
Yield: 6 1/2 dozen puffs

Chocolate-Mint Filling

 2 squares (1 ounce each)
    unsweetened baking
    chocolate
 2/3 cup butter, softened
 1 cup sugar
 1/2 teaspoon vanilla extract
 1/8 teaspoon peppermint extract
 1/2 cup egg substitute, divided

Melt chocolate in a small heavy saucepan over low heat; cool to room temperature.

Beat butter at medium speed with an electric mixer until creamy; gradually add sugar and beat 5 to 7 minutes. Add chocolate and extracts, beating at low speed until blended.

Add 1/4 cup egg substitute; beat 5 minutes. Add remaining 1/4 cup egg substitute and beat 5 additional minutes.
Yield: about 3 cups filling

SNOW DUDE

(shown on page 71)

You will need tracing paper; green, orange, blue, and furry white fleece; polyester fiberfill; fabric glue; orange, green, and black embroidery floss; 1" dia. green buttons; ¼" dia. black shank buttons; and pink blush or chalk.

Snow Dude is designed for children ages 3 and up. Match right sides and raw edges and use a ¼" seam allowance for all sewing.

1. Enlarge the snowman pattern, page 180, to 155%. Trace the remaining patterns, pages 179–180, onto tracing paper. Cut four mittens (two in reverse) and four boots (two in reverse) from green fleece. Cut a nose from orange fleece. Cut two snowman shapes from white fleece. Mark the arm and leg openings as shown on the pattern.
2. Cut two 2" x 11" and two 2" x 15" strips from blue fleece for the arms and legs.
3. Matching the long edges, fold each strip in half; stitch. Turn each tube right side out.
4. Matching the raw edges and opening marks, tack the arm and leg tubes to the right side of the snowman back. Bunch up the tubes and pin them to the middle of the back piece.
5. Leaving an opening at the top for turning, sew the snowman front and back together. Turn right side out; unpin. Sew the green buttons to the body with green floss. Stuff with fiberfill and sew the opening closed.

Knot each arm at the elbow and each leg at the knee.
6. Leaving the tops open, sew the mitten and boot pairs together; clip the curves and turn them right side out. Fold the mitten and boot tops ½" to the inside and glue the arm and leg ends inside the mittens and boots.
7. For the scarf, cut one 2" x 30" strip each from blue and orange fleece. Sew the strips together along the long edges. Turn the scarf right side out and sew across the ends 2" from each edge. Cut ⅜"w fringe on each end and tie the scarf around the neck.
8. For the hat, cut one 8" x 16" piece each from blue and orange fleece. Sew the ends of the blue piece together to form a tube; repeat with the orange piece. Turn the orange tube right side out. Matching seams and edges, insert the orange tube in the blue tube. Sew the tubes together along the bottom edge; turn the hat right side out. Using six strands of orange floss, sew *Running Stitches*, page 185, 2½" from the top of the hat through both layers. Pull the floss tight and wrap it around the gathers; knot to secure. Cut ½"w fringe at the top. Turn the cuff up and tack the hat to the head.
9. Sew the black buttons to the face. Glue the nose and a black floss mouth to the face. Add cheeks with blush or chalk.

KNIT STOCKING

(shown on page 72)

Refer to Knit and Crochet, page 186, before beginning the project.

■■■□ INTERMEDIATE

Finished Size:
6¼"w x 19"l
(16 cm x 48.5 cm)

You will need 1 skein each of Red, Green, and Ecru, Medium Weight Yarn [7 ounces, 364 yards (198 grams, 333 meters) per skein]; straight knitting needles, size 8 (5 mm) **or** size needed for gauge; 3 stitch holders; yarn needle; tin alphabet stars; wooden beads; and jump rings.

Gauge:
In pattern, 19 sts and 36 rows = 4" (10 cm)

CUFF

With Ecru, cast on 66 sts.
Rows 1-3: (K1, P1) across.
Row 4 (Right side): With Green knit across.
Row 5: (K1, P1) across.
Row 6: With Ecru knit across.
Row 7: (K1, P1) across.
Rows 8-10: Repeat Rows 4-6.
Rows 11 and 12: (K1, P1) across.
Note: Place a marker in the stitch at each end of the last row.
Rows 13-24: (K1, P1) across.

LEG

Row 1: With Green increase *(see Increases, page 186)*, knit across: 67 sts.
Row 2: Knit across.
Row 3: With Red, slip 1 as if to purl, (K1, slip 1 as if to **purl**) across.
Row 4: K1, (WYF slip 1 as if to **purl**, K1) across.
Rows 5 and 6: With Ecru knit across.
Row 7: With Green, slip 1 as if to **purl**, (K1, slip 1 as if to **purl**) across.
Row 8: K1, (WYF slip 1 as if to **purl**, K1) across.
Rows 9 and 10: With Red knit across.
Row 11: With Ecru slip 1 as if to **purl**, (K1, slip 1 as if to **purl**) across.

continued on page 154

Row 12: K1, (WYF slip 1 as if to **purl**, K1) across.
Rows 13 and 14: With Green knit across.
Repeat Rows 3-14 until piece measures approximately 15" (38 cm) from cast on edge, ending by working Row 4.

Cut Red and Green.

HEEL
FIRST HALF
Row 1: With Ecru, K13, K2 tog (*Fig. 1, page 186*), K1, slip next 35 sts onto st holder (Instep), slip remaining 16 sts onto second st holder (Heel):15 sts.
Row 2: Purl across.
Row 3 (Decrease row): Knit across to last 3 sts, K2 tog, K1: 14 sts.
Row 4: Purl across.
Rows 5-16: Repeat Rows 3 and 4, 6 times: 8 sts.
Row 17: Knit across, pick up one st in end of Row 16 (*Fig. 6, page 187*): 9 sts.
Row 18: Purl across.
Row 19 (Increase row): Knit across, skip next row, pick up one st in next row: 10 sts.
Row 20: Purl across.
Rows 21- 32: Repeat Rows 19 and 20, 6 times: 16 sts.

Cut Ecru; slip sts onto st holder.

SECOND HALF
Row 1 (Decrease row): Slip 16 sts from heel st holder onto empty needle, with Ecru, K1, SSK (*Figs. 3a–c, page 187*), knit across: 15 sts.
Row 2: Purl across.
Rows 3-16: Repeat Rows 1 and 2, 7 times: 8 sts.
Row 17: Knit across.
Row 18: Purl across, pick up one st in Row 16 (*Fig. 7, page 187*): 9 sts.
Row 19: Knit across.

Row 20 (Increase row): Purl across, skip next row, pick up one st in next row: 10 sts.
Rows 21-32: Repeat Rows 19 and 20, 6 times: 16 sts.
Cut yarn.
Slip Instep sts onto same needle as Second Half of Heel, then slip sts from First Half of Heel onto same needle: 67 sts.

INSTEP
Rows 1 and 2: With Ecru knit across.
Row 3: With Green, slip 1 as if to **purl**, (K1, slip 1 as if to **purl**) 7 times, K2 tog, slip 1 as if to **purl**, (K1, slip 1 as if to **purl**) 16 times, SSK, slip 1 as if to **purl**, (K1, slip 1 as if to **purl**) across: 65 sts.
Row 4: K1, (WYF slip 1 as if to **purl**, K1) across.
Row 5: With Red K 14, K2 tog, K 33, SSK, knit across: 63 sts.
Row 6: Knit across.
Row 7: With Ecru, slip 1 as if to **purl**, (K1, slip 1 as if to **purl**) 6 times, K2 tog, slip 1 as if to **purl**, (K1, slip 1 as if to **purl**) 16 times, SSK, slip 1 as if to **purl**, (K1, slip 1 as if to **purl**) across: 61 sts.
Row 8: K1, (WYF slip 1 as if to **purl**, K1) across.
Row 9: With Green K 12, K2 tog, K 33, SSK, knit across: 59 sts.
Row 10: Knit across.
Repeat Rows 3-14 of Leg (*see page 153*) until Instep measures 4¹⁄₂" (11.5 cm), ending by working Row 9.
Last Row: K 14, (K2 tog, K 13) 3 times: 56 sts.

Cut Red and Green.

TOE
Row 1: With Ecru K 11, SSK, K2, K2 tog, K 22, SSK, K2, K2 tog, K 11: 52 sts.
Row 2: Purl across.
Row 3: K 10, SSK, K2, K2 tog, K 20, SSK, K2, K2 tog, K 10: 48 sts.

Row 4: Purl across.
Row 5: K9, SSK, K2, K2 tog, K 18, SSK, K2, K2 tog, K9: 44 sts.
Row 6: Purl across.
Row 7: K8, SSK, K2, K2 tog, K 16, SSK, K2, K2 tog, K8: 40 sts.
Row 8: Purl across.
Row 9: K7, SSK, K2, K2 tog, K 14, SSK, K2, K2 tog, K7: 36 sts.
Row 10: Purl across.
Row 11: K6, SSK, K2, K2 tog, K 12, SSK, K2, K2 tog, K6: 32 sts.
Row 12: Purl across.
Row 13: K5, SSK, K2, K2 tog, K8, SSK, K2, K2 tog, K5: 28 sts.
Row 14: Purl across.
Row 15: K2 tog across: 14 sts.

Cut yarn, leaving a long end for sewing. Thread yarn needle with long end, weave needle through remaining sts, gathering tightly, and secure end. With **right** sides facing you, weave seam to marker sts (*Fig. 8, page 187*); then with **wrong** side facing you, weave remaining seam. If desired, sew opening at Heel gusset closed.

SNOWMAN SLIPPERS
(shown on page 71)

You will need a pair of slippers; tracing paper; white, orange, and black felt; matching embroidery floss; and snowflake buttons.

1. For each slipper, use the patterns, page 179, and cut out the head, nose, mouth, and eye shapes from felt.
2. Use three strands of the appropriate floss colors and *Whipstitch*, page 185, the shapes in place on each slipper.
3. Sew the snowflake buttons to the slippers.

BEADED NECKLACE & EARRINGS

(shown on page 73)

For the necklace, you will need ¼"w silver foil tape, flat tumbled glass piece, solder and soldering tool, 6mm split ring, green rainbow glass bead mix, 24-gauge silver wire, wire cutters, needle-nose pliers, silver tiger tail jewelry wire, green opaque glass bead mix, silver seed beads, 6mm jump rings, silver S-shaped clasp, and silver crimp beads.

For the earrings, you will need 24-gauge silver wire, wire cutters, two tumbled glass pieces, two silver spacer beads, and two silver French ear wires.

Necklace

1. Remove the paper backing and wrap the foil tape around the edges of the glass piece; overlap and solder the ends. Solder the split ring to the top edge of the glass piece.
2. Adding rainbow beads as desired, wrap the glass piece with 24-gauge wire and use the pliers to coil the ends around the wrapped wire to secure.
3. Cut three lengths of tiger tail wire 4" longer than the desired length of the necklace. Thread the glass piece onto the center of the lengths. Leaving 2½" unbeaded on each end, thread rainbow, opaque, and seed beads each on a separate strand. Twist the strands around each other.

4. Thread one wire end of the rainbow strand through a crimp bead, a jump ring, and back through the crimp bead. Use the pliers to crimp the bead; trim the wire end. Repeat with the silver and opaque strands, using the same jump ring for all three strands.
5. Thread the loose end of the rainbow strand through a crimp bead, twice around one end of the S-shaped clasp, and back through the crimp bead. Use the pliers to crimp the bead; trim the wire end. Repeat with the silver and opaque strands.

Earrings

1. For each earring, randomly wrap a length of wire around a glass piece, coiling one end under the wire at the front to secure.
2. Thread the remaining wire end through a spacer bead, through the loop on the ear wire, and back through the bead. Twist the end around the wire at the back of the glass piece; trim and tuck the end.

HOLIDAY BOX

(shown on page 70)

You will need sandpaper, tack cloth, primer, 5¾" x 6¼" x 4" wooden box with a hinged lid, black and assorted colors of acrylic paint, paintbrushes, tracing paper, transfer paper, clear acrylic glaze, drill, and a glass drawer knob.

Allow primer, paint, and glaze to dry after each application. Apply additional coats as needed.

1. Sand, then wipe the box with the tack cloth. Prime, then paint the box black.

2. Trace, then transfer the patterns, pages 181–182, onto the top and sides of the box.
3. Paint the designs as desired.
4. Apply a thick layer of glaze to the box.
5. Drill a hole through the center of the lid and attach the knob.

HOT DOG NECK WARMER

(shown on page 73)

You will need two pairs of tightly knit hunting socks, polyester fiberfill, dark brown embroidery floss, tracing paper, scraps of black and red wool felt, ⅜"w red ribbon, and rice.

Refer to Embroidery, page 185, before beginning the project. Use three strands of floss for all embroidery and use a ½" seam allowance for all sewing. Heat the completed neck warmer for 2 minutes in the microwave.

1. For the dog's head, cut the foot from one sock just past the heel; fill it with fiberfill. Use floss to tie the neck end of the sock closed.
2. Use the patterns, page 179, and cut the eyes and tongue from felt. Use floss to *Whipstitch* the eyes to the head. Tack the tongue to the head. To form the nose, sew a folded length of ribbon to the head.
3. For the body, fill one sock with rice. Work *Running Stitches* around the open end of the body, slip the dog's neck in the opening, and pull tightly to gather; knot and trim the thread ends. *Whipstitch* the body to the neck. Tie a bow around the neck.

continued on page 156

4. For the ears, cut the feet from the remaining socks just below the heels; turn wrong side out. Work *Running Stitches* around the open end of each foot and pull tightly to gather; knot the thread ends. *Whipstitch* the ears to the head.

5. For the front legs, turn a sock tube wrong side out. Trim the tube to the desired length plus ½". Sew one end of the tube closed. Refer to Fig. 1 to sew two lines of stitching; then, cut the tube in half between the lines. Turn each piece right side out and fill it with fiberfill. *Whipstitch* the legs to the body.

Fig. 1

6. Repeat Step 5 for the back legs and use the remaining tube to add a stuffed tail to the body.

7. Work *Straight Stitches* to add toes to the end of each leg.

GIFTS FOR EVERY TASTE

CANDY CLIPBOARDS
(shown on page 76)

For each clipboard, you will need scrapbook paper, 6" x 9" clipboard, spray adhesive, colored markers, cardstock, scallop-edged craft scissors, candy-filled cellophane bag, double-sided tape, and ribbon.

Use spray adhesive in a well-ventilated area.

1. Tear and trim scrapbook paper to fit the front of the clipboard. Spray the back of the paper with adhesive and apply it to the board.

2. Photocopy the recipe and label patterns, page 184; cut them out. Color the designs, adhere them to cardstock, and trim with craft scissors.

3. Adhere the recipe to the bottom of the clipboard. Clip the bag on the board. Tape a ribbon loop on the back of the label and tape the label to the bag.

COOL YULE COOKIE BAGS
(shown on page 77)

You will need blue cardstock, snowflake vellum, 5"w plastic zipping bag, cookie, wavy-edged craft scissors, white ink pad, iridescent embossing powder, heat embossing tool, hole punch, snowflake brads, alphabet stickers, craft glue, and fibers.

Use caution when working with the heat embossing tool.

1. Cut a cardstock and vellum piece to fit in the bag. With the vellum on top, place the pieces in the bag. Slip the cookie in front of the vellum and close the bag.

2. For the label, fold a 5" cardstock square in half. Trim the front edge with craft scissors. Ink along the trimmed edge and sprinkle it with embossing powder. Follow the manufacturer's instructions to heat-set the powder.

3. Cut a vellum tag. Fold the label over the zipper-end of the bag. Punch holes for the brad prongs. Use the brads to attach the label and tag to the bag. Add a sticker message and glue fibers to the label and tag.

SYRUP CONTAINER
(shown on page 77)

You will need white air-dry modeling clay, rubber stamp (we used a Santa stamp with a square rubber background for a better impression), fine-point markers, wavy-edged craft scissors, cardstock, craft glue, adhesive-backed magnetic strip, double-sided tape, ribbons, syrup container, glue dot, alphabet stamps, distressed ink pad, striped scrapbook paper, and a hole punch.

1. Flatten the clay to ¼" thickness. Stamp the image and trim the clay. Allow to dry; then, color the image.

2. Use the craft scissors to cut a cardstock piece larger than the stamped piece; glue it to the back. Apply the magnet to the back of the cardstock.

3. Tape ribbon around the container. Attach the magnet to the ribbon with the glue dot.

4. Stamp the scrapbook paper as shown. Cut the paper into a tag and glue it to cardstock. Trim the cardstock slightly larger than the tag. Punch a hole in the tag and tie it to the handle with a ribbon bow.

CUPCAKE PICKS AND WRAP-AROUNDS
(shown on page 78)

You will need 1¼" and 1½" dia. circle punches, cardstock, scrapbook papers, craft glue, ⅛" dia. hole punch, silver and red chenille stems, satin cord, assorted white pom-poms, and cupcakes.

1. Punch cardstock and paper circles. For each favor, glue two punched circles together. Punch a hole through opposite sides of each layered circle.
2. For each pick, thread a silver stem through the holes. Bend one end to the front of the circle to secure and bend the other end into a zigzag pick. For each wrap-around, thread a 12"-long cord through the holes.
3. For each snowman, glue three pom-poms together. Tie a red chenille "scarf" around the neck and glue a cardstock hat to the head. Glue the snowman to a pick or wrap-around.
4. Insert the picks and knot the cord ends around the cupcakes.

POUND CAKE LOAFPANS
(shown on page 78)

You will need white, blue, and red cardstock; mini foil loafpans; craft glue; rub-on letters; snowflake punch; double-sided tape; ribbon; tracing paper; black fine-point marker; hole punch; chenille stems; cellophane; and faceted beads.

1. Cut a white cardstock label for one long side of each pan and glue it to blue cardstock. Trim the blue piece larger than the label.
2. Add rub-ons and glue punched snowflakes to the label. Tape ribbon around the pan and tape the label on one side.
3. Use the patterns, page 183, and cut the shapes from cardstock. Write "Cherry Pound Cake" on the cherries and glue them to the tag. Punch a hole in the tag. Twist two chenille stems together and thread one through the hole in the tag.
4. Gather cellophane around the pan and secure with the chenille stems. Add beads to the stem ends.

SAUCE JAR
(shown on page 79)

You will need a pint canning jar with a lid, adhesive-backed craft foam sheets, 1"w and 2"w foam tree stickers, glue pen, red beads, foam alphabet stickers, red craft foam, fine-point marker, hole punch, and a gold cord.

1. Draw around the inner lid of the jar onto adhesive foam and cut it out. Adhere the circle to the lid and place the lid on the jar. Apply the large tree sticker to the lid and glue beads on the tree.
2. Apply alphabet stickers to a 2½" x 3½" adhesive foam label. Adhere the label to the jar.
3. Cut a 1½" x 3" red foam tag. Apply the small tree sticker to the tag and add a message. Punch a hole in the end. Use the cord to tie the tag around the jar lid.

DECORATED NUT CAN
(shown on page 79)

You will need coordinating scrapbook papers; 3"h x 4" dia. nut can with a lid; craft glue; red, green, and white cardstock; scallop-edged craft scissors; rub-on letters; tracing paper; spray adhesive; light green, green, and red glitter; and a ¼" dia. hole punch.

Use spray adhesive in a well-ventilated area.

1. Cut a scrapbook paper strip to cover the can and a circle to fit on the lid; glue in place. Cut a slightly smaller circle from cardstock and glue it to the lid.
2. Cut a 1½"w scrapbook paper strip to fit around the can. Use craft scissors to cut a slightly wider strip from white cardstock. Stack and glue the strips on the can.
3. Cut four 1¾" cardstock squares and four 2⅛" scrapbook paper squares. Stack and glue the squares on the can with the side points of three squares touching and the remaining square centered on the back. Label the center front square with rub-ons.
4. Trace the patterns, page 183, and cut four peppers and caps from green cardstock. Punch six circles from red cardstock. Spray the shapes with adhesive; apply glitter, allow to dry, and shake off the excess. Glue the peppers to the remaining squares and the lid. Glue the circles over the side points of the squares.

POPCORN PAIL
(shown on page 80)

You will need red and white cardstock, wavy-edged craft scissors, red-checked and green scrapbook papers, double-sided tape, new one-gallon paint can with a lid, fine-point permanent marker, acetate sheet, permanent oil-based paint marker, golden brown chalk, adhesive foam dots, cork alphabet circles, alphabet stickers, rub-on letters, hole punch, and assorted ribbons.

1. For the label, cut a 5" dia. red cardstock circle. Use craft scissors to cut slightly larger and smaller scrapbook paper circles. Stack and tape the circles on the lid.
2. Use the fine-point marker to trace the patterns, page 183, onto acetate; cut them out.
3. For the tag, use the patterns and cut the "bag" pieces from cardstock and scrapbook papers. Trim the top of the bag with craft scissors.
4. Tape the popcorn patterns to the can and draw around them with the paint marker. Reposition and repeat as desired.
5. Cut several popcorn pieces from white cardstock. Chalk the pieces. Tape a popcorn piece to the lid and the top edge of the tag. Use foam dots to attach the remaining pieces to the can, lid, and tag.
6. Add alphabet circles, stickers, and rub-ons to the label. Add names to the tag with the fine-point marker. Punch a hole in the top of the tag.
7. Use ribbon to tie the tag to around a piece of popcorn on the lid. Wrap ribbon around the handle and knot the ends. Tie additional ribbons at each end of the handle.

SEASONING SACK
(shown on page 80)

You will need red and cream cardstock, plaid and striped scrapbook papers, wavy-edged craft scissors, plastic zipping bag filled with seasoning, hole punch, letter dies and a die-cutting tool, craft glue, alphabet stamps, black and green ink pads, red pen, adhesive foam dots, and red ribbon.

1. For the sack, cut a 7" x 11" red cardstock piece. Fold 4¹/₂" from each short end; unfold.
2. For the topper, match long edges and fold a 4" x 7" plaid paper piece in half. Trim the long edges with craft scissors.
3. Place the plastic bag in the sack, aligning the top edges. Place the topper over the top of the sack and punch two holes through all layers.
4. Die-cut "tex-mex" from cream cardstock. Glue the letters and a striped paper strip to the front of the sack. Stamp "seasoning" on the paper strip.
5. For each tree, press green-inked fingers onto cream cardstock in a tier shape. Draw a red star, trunk, and dots; then, cut around the fingerprints in the shape of a tree. Glue one tree to the sack and adhere two trees with foam dots.
6. Use ribbon to tie the sack pieces together.

BAKING MIX CANISTER
(shown on page 81)

You will need jumbo rickrack; assorted fibers; plastic 13-cup canister; tracing paper; white, blue, and dark blue cardstock; palette knife; Snow-Tex™ Textural Medium; hole punch; craft glue; orange bead; two black buttons; and a white gel pen.

1. Tie rickrack and fibers around the canister.
2. Use the pattern, page 183, and cut a snowman from cardstock. Use the palette knife to apply Snow-Tex to the snowman and allow to dry.
3. Braid fibers together for the scarf and knot the ends. Tie the scarf around the neck. Cut a blue fiber mouth and punch eyes from cardstock. Glue the eyes, mouth, bead nose, and buttons on the snowman.
4. Glue the snowman on a 5" cardstock square. Add gel pen snowflakes.
5. Cut a 5" cardstock square for each recipe. Write or print the recipes on the squares. Stack the squares with the snowman on top and punch a hole through all layers. Tie the squares to the canister.

PATTERNS

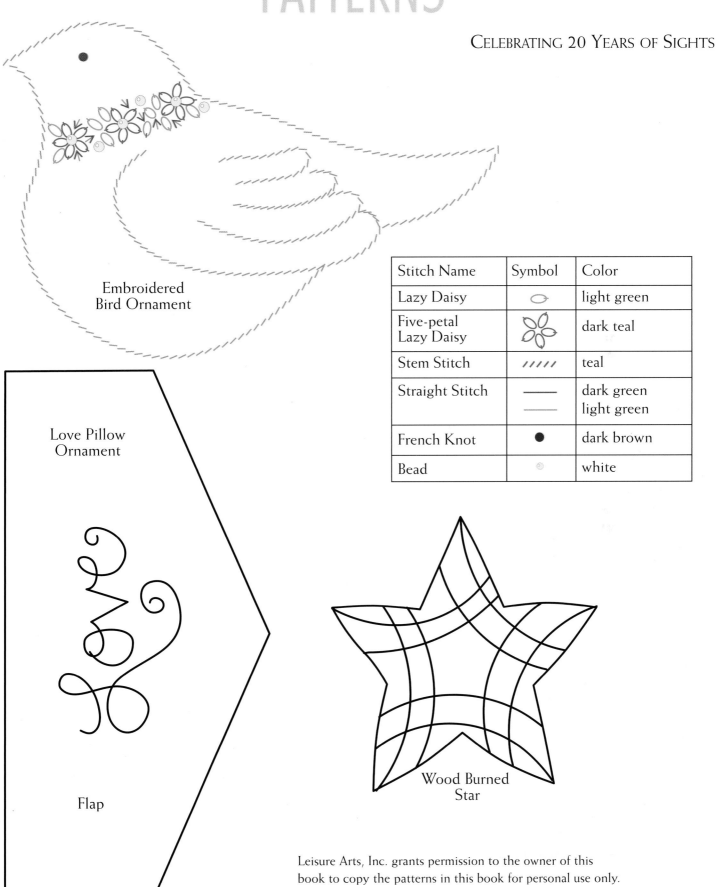

Embroidered
Bird Ornament

Stitch Name	Symbol	Color
Lazy Daisy	⬭	light green
Five-petal Lazy Daisy	🌸	dark teal
Stem Stitch	/////	teal
Straight Stitch	——	dark green
	——	light green
French Knot	●	dark brown
Bead	◎	white

Love Pillow
Ornament

Flap

Wood Burned
Star

Leisure Arts, Inc. grants permission to the owner of this
book to copy the patterns in this book for personal use only.

Folk-Art Appliquéd
Ornament

Crocheted
Snowflake

Mitten

Hat

Penguin

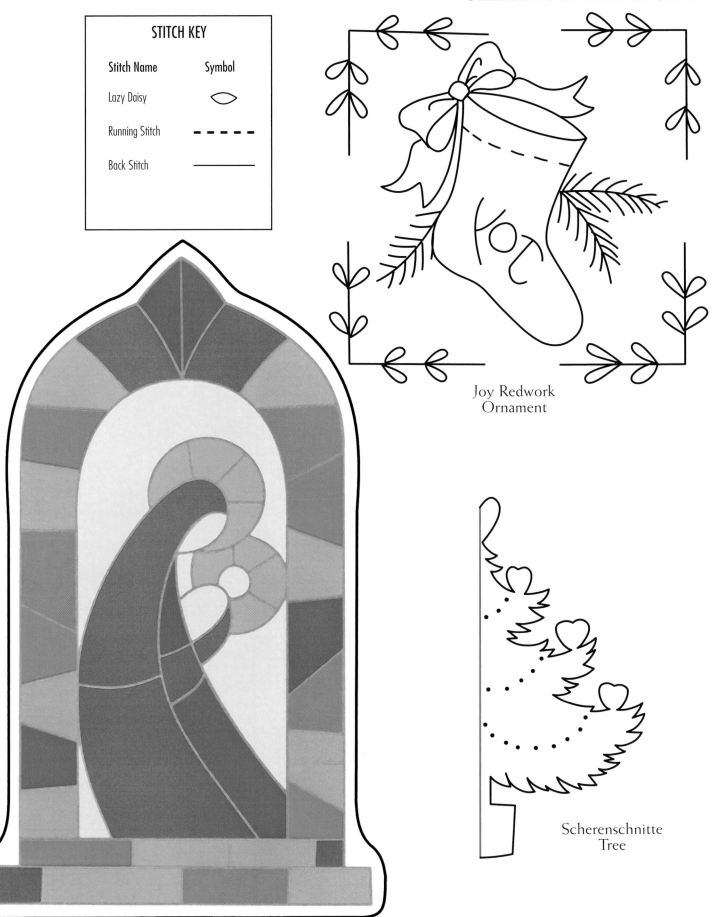

STITCH KEY

Stitch Name	Symbol
Lazy Daisy	
Running Stitch	
Back Stitch	

Joy Redwork
Ornament

Scherenschnitte
Tree

Madonna and Child

Large Point
(cut 5)

Small Point
(cut 5)

Hanging
Tin Star

crimp this edge

crimp this edge

crimp this edge

crimp this edge

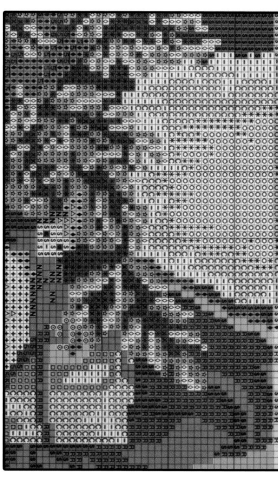

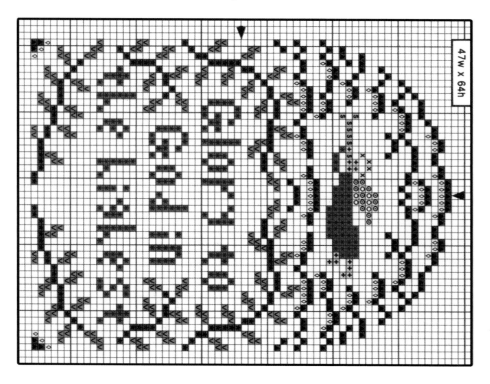

47w x 64h

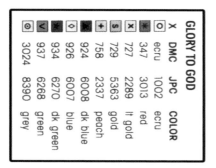

	DMC	JPC	COLOR
X	ecru	ecru	ecru
⊙	1002		
⊙	347	3013	red
V	727	2289	lt gold
▨	729	5363	gold
▣	758	2337	peach
▦	924	6008	dk blue
+	926	6007	blue
S	934	6270	dk green
X	937	6268	green
✳	3024	8390	grey

GLORY TO GOD

Glory
to God

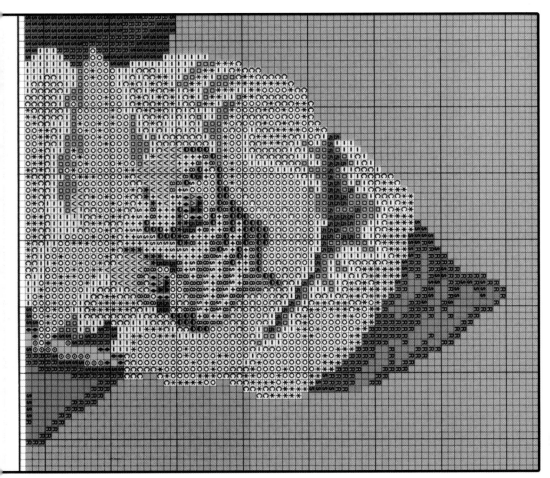

Santa Door
Hanger

SANTA DOOR HANGER (69w x 119h)	
PATERNAYAN	**COLOR**
220	black
261	ecru
262	cream
461	vy dk beige
462	dk beige
463	beige
464	lt beige
465	vy lt beige
486	vy dk flesh
490	dk flesh
491	flesh
492	lt flesh
493	vy lt flesh
511	dk blue
512	blue
513	lt blue
515	vy lt blue
534	blue green
661	dk green
662	green
663	lt green
730	brown
733	dk gold
734	gold
735	lt gold
901	dk red
933	dk pink
934	pink
940	red
941	lt red

Grey area indicates last row of top section of design.

Scherenschnitte
Reindeer

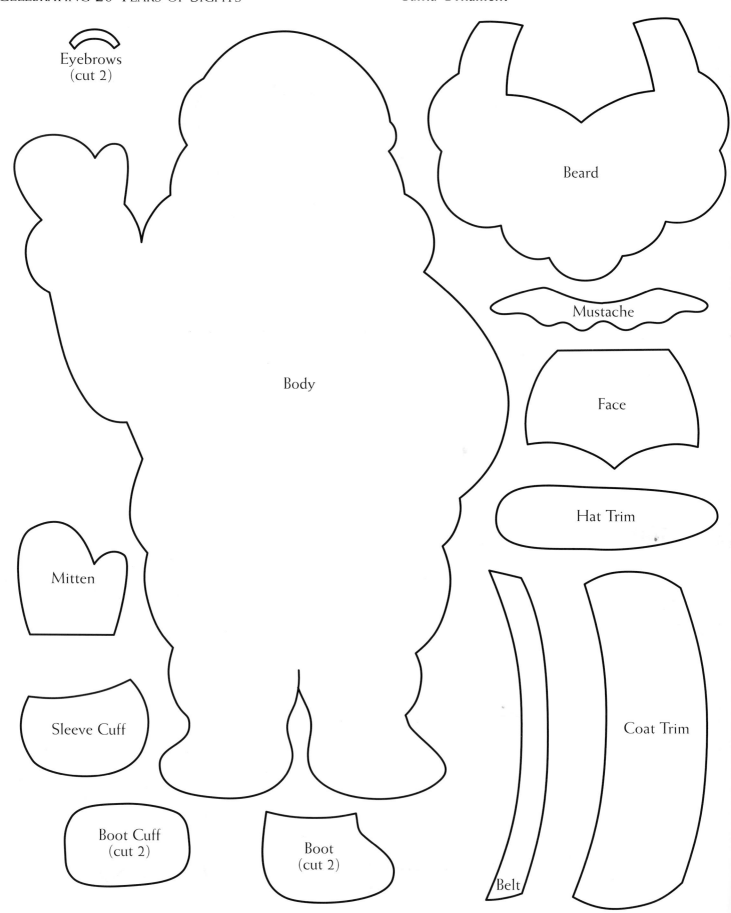

Eyebrows
(cut 2)

Beard

Mustache

Body

Face

Hat Trim

Mitten

Coat Trim

Sleeve Cuff

Boot Cuff
(cut 2)

Boot
(cut 2)

Belt

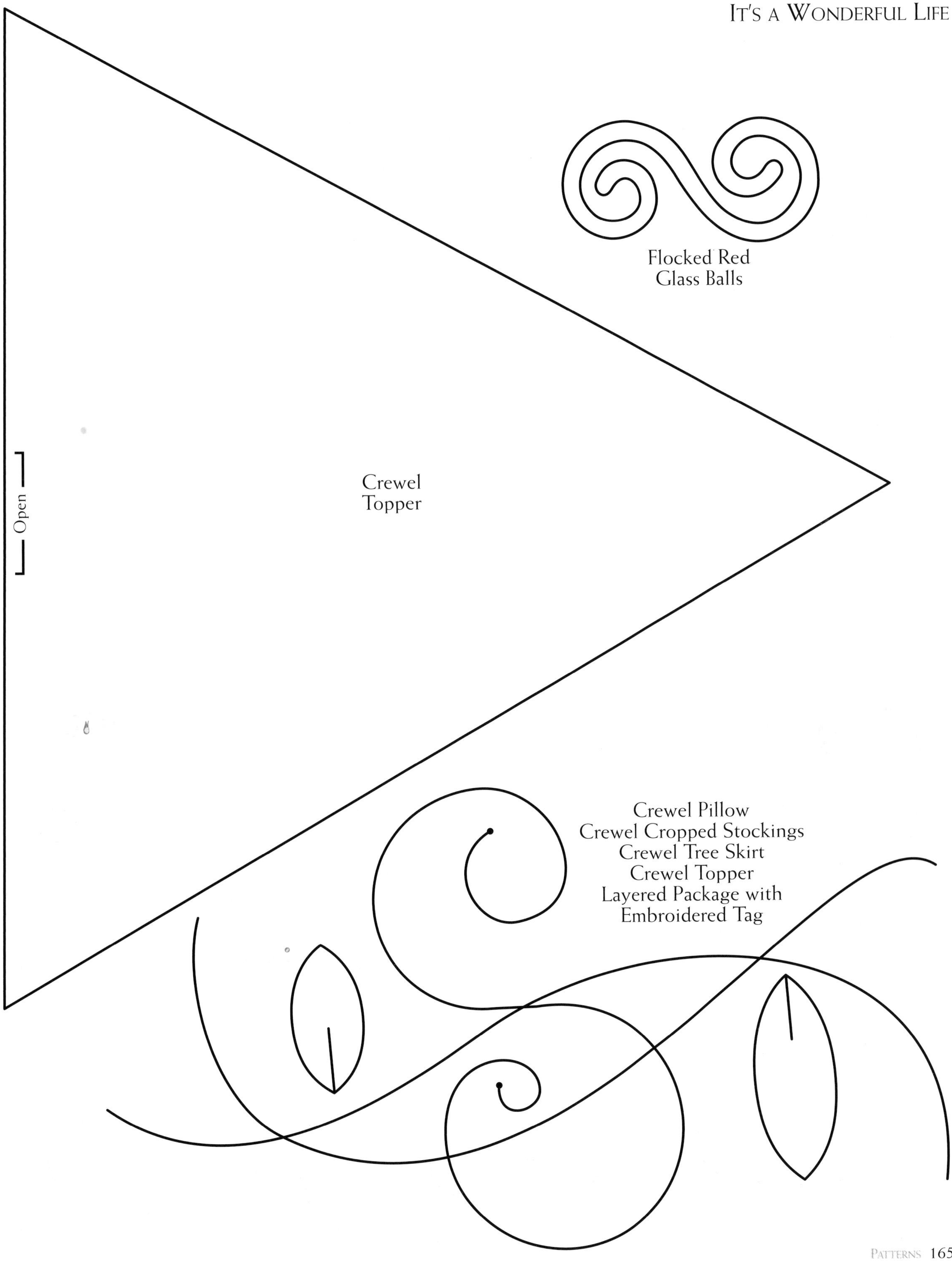

Flocked Red
Glass Balls

Open

Crewel
Topper

Crewel Pillow
Crewel Cropped Stockings
Crewel Tree Skirt
Crewel Topper
Layered Package with
Embroidered Tag

Glittery
Cardstock
Snowflake

Snowman
Ornament

Snowflake
Garland

Glittery Newsprint
Snowflake
&
Snowflake Tree
Topper

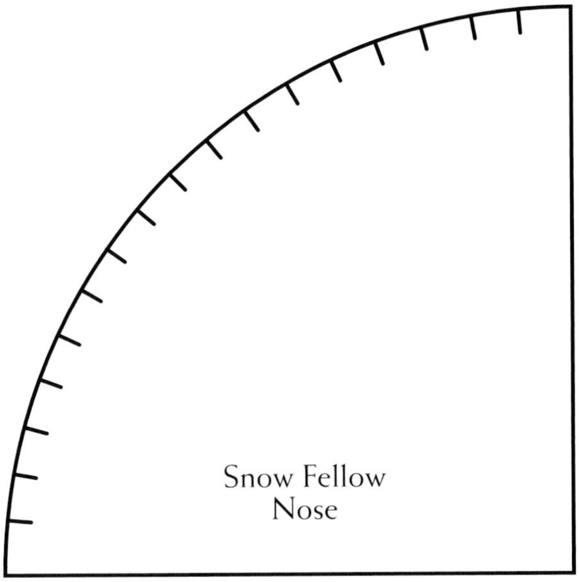

Snow Fellow
Nose

Snow Fellow
Mitten

A BEACH HOUSE CHRISTMAS

Tag
Advent
Calendar

Wrapped
Candle Holder

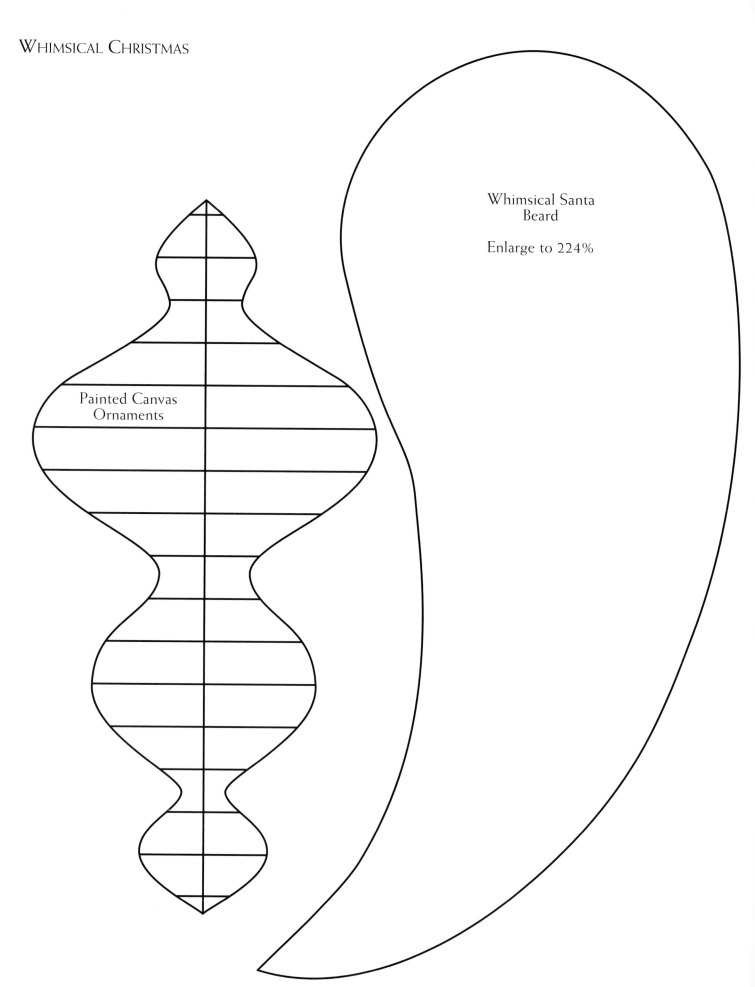

Whimsical Santa
Beard

Enlarge to 224%

Painted Canvas
Ornaments

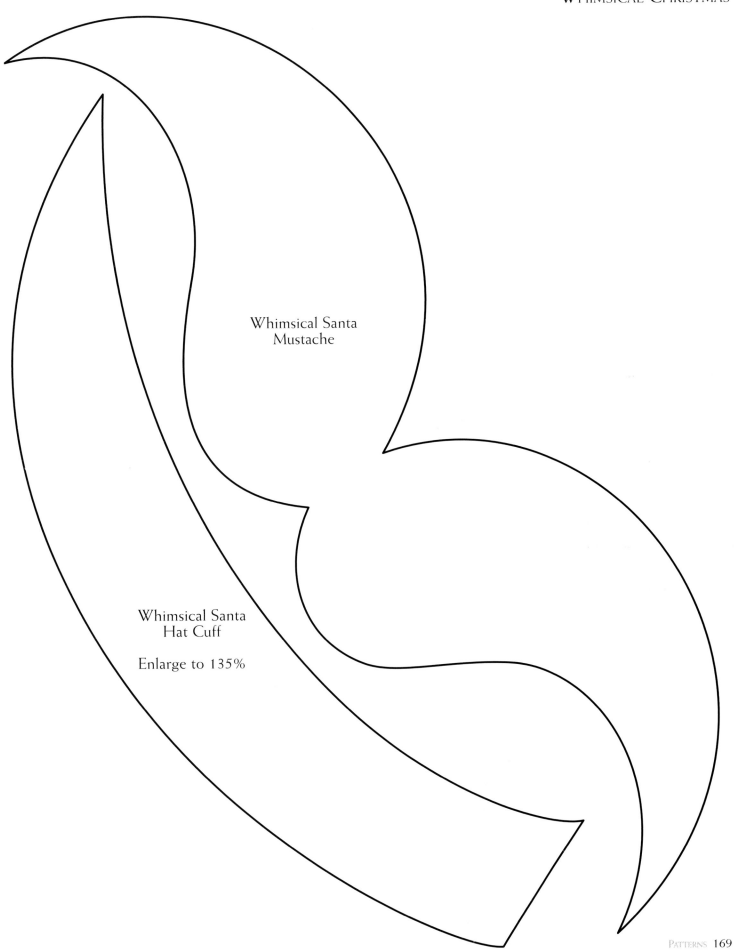

Whimsical Santa
Mustache

Whimsical Santa
Hat Cuff

Enlarge to 135%

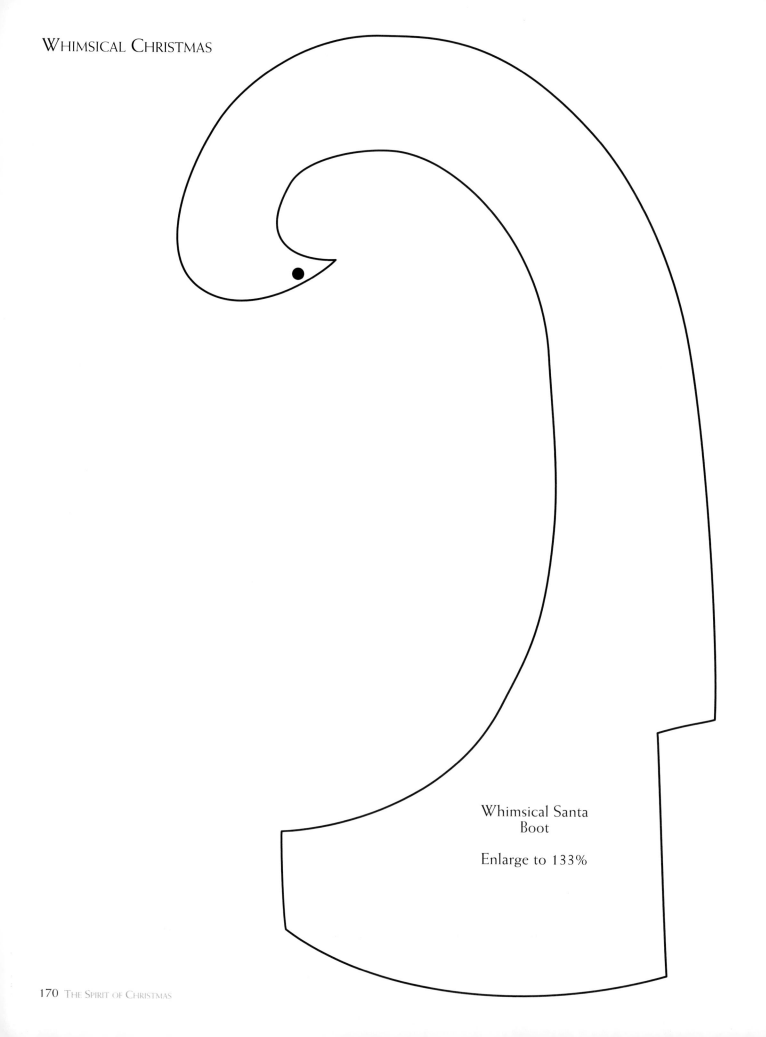

Whimsical Santa
Boot

Enlarge to 133%

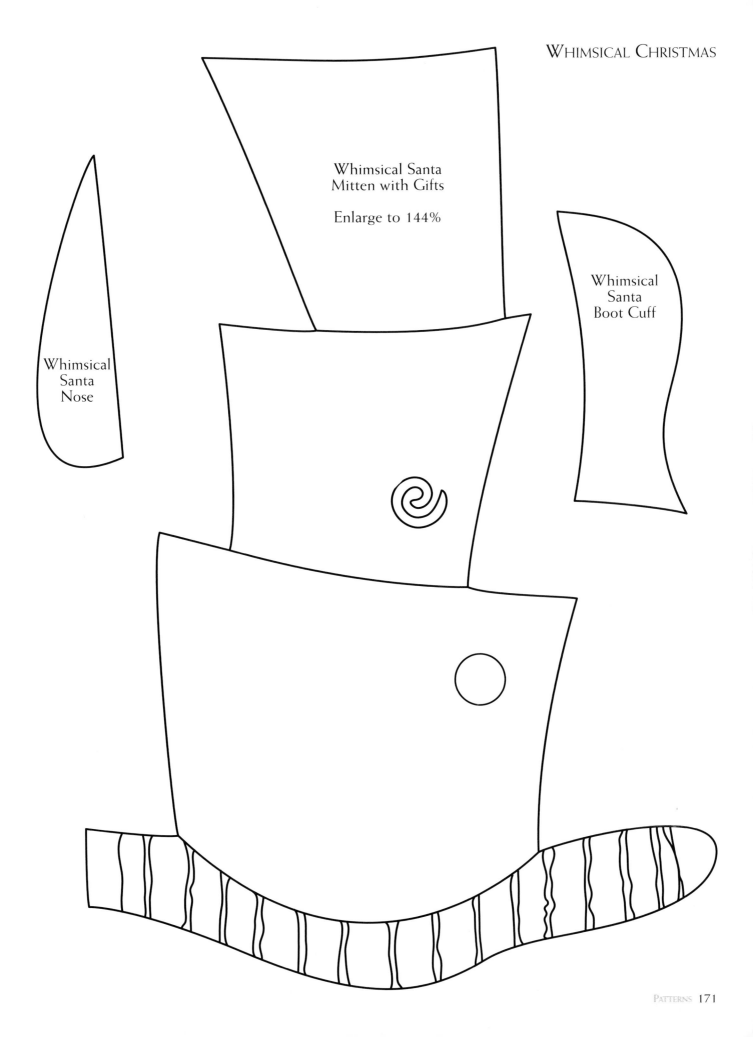

Whimsical Santa
Mitten with Gifts

Enlarge to 144%

Whimsical
Santa
Boot Cuff

Whimsical
Santa
Nose

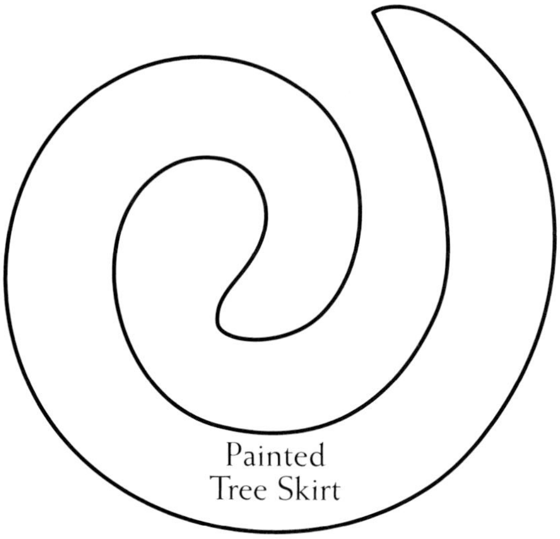

Painted
Tree Skirt

Painted
Tree Skirt

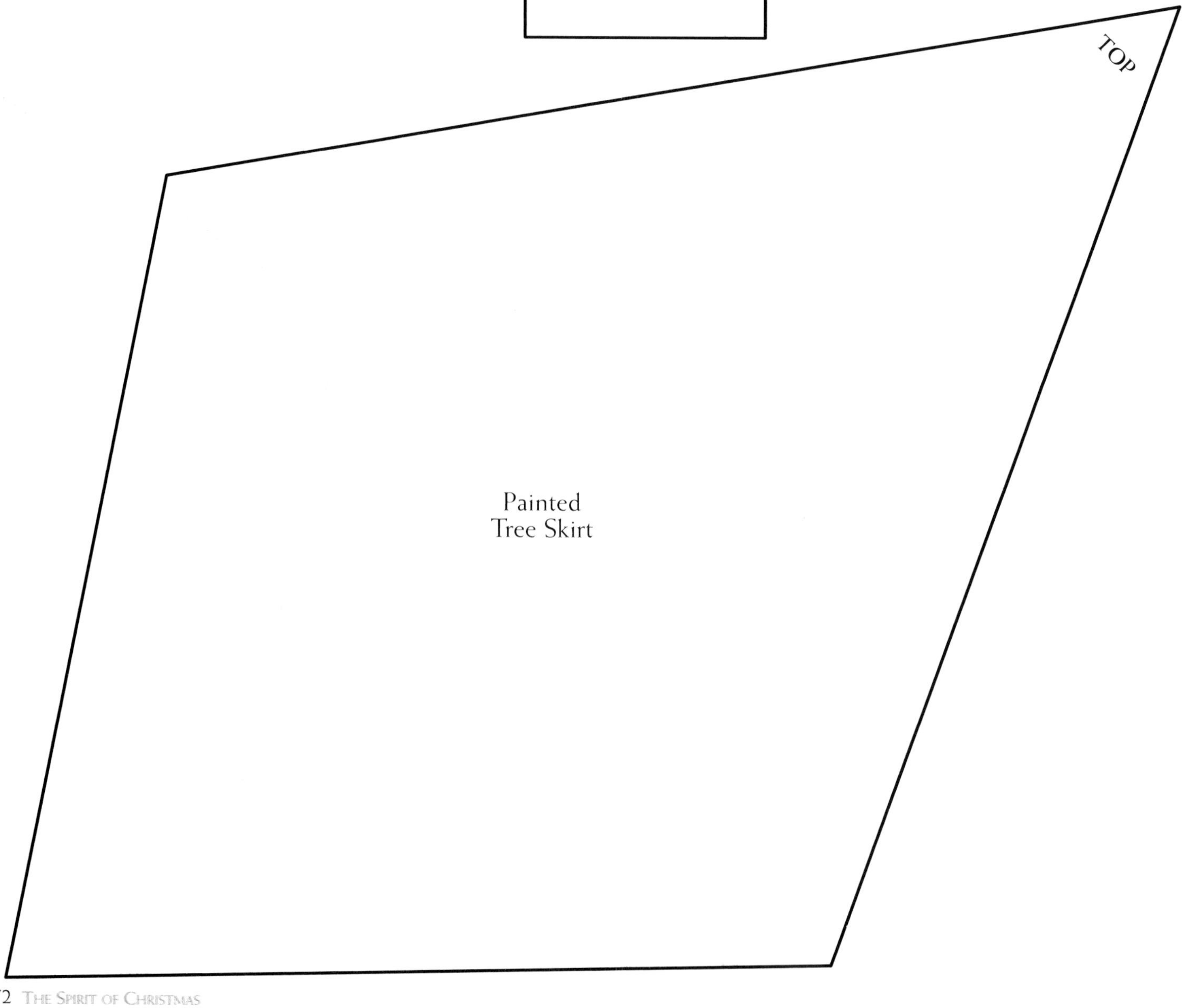

Painted
Tree Skirt

TOP

Painted
Tree Skirt

TOP

Star Tree
Topper

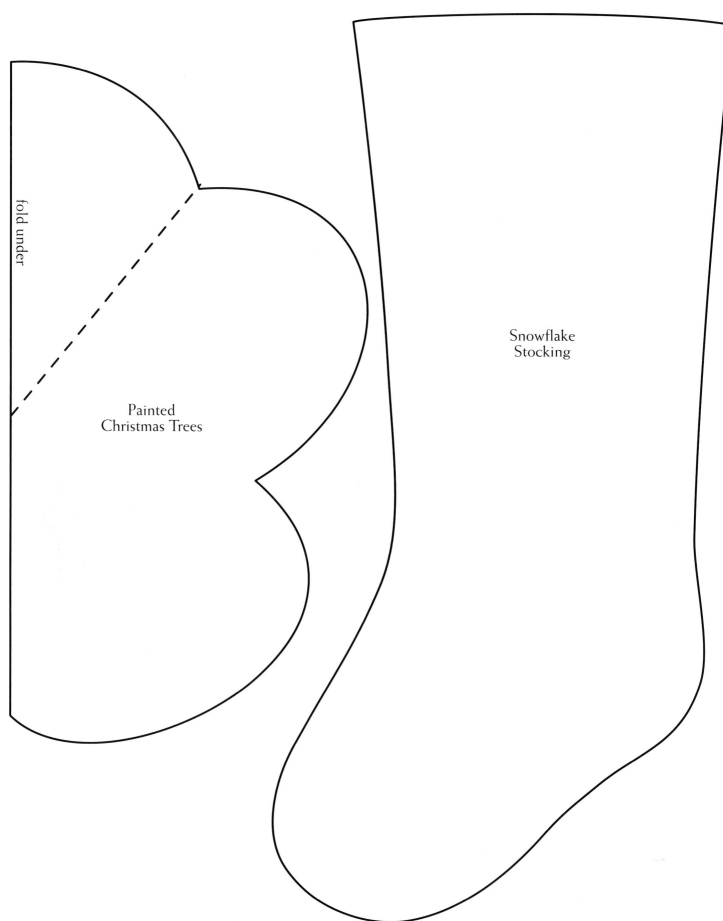

fold under

Painted
Christmas Trees

Snowflake
Stocking

Framed Angels

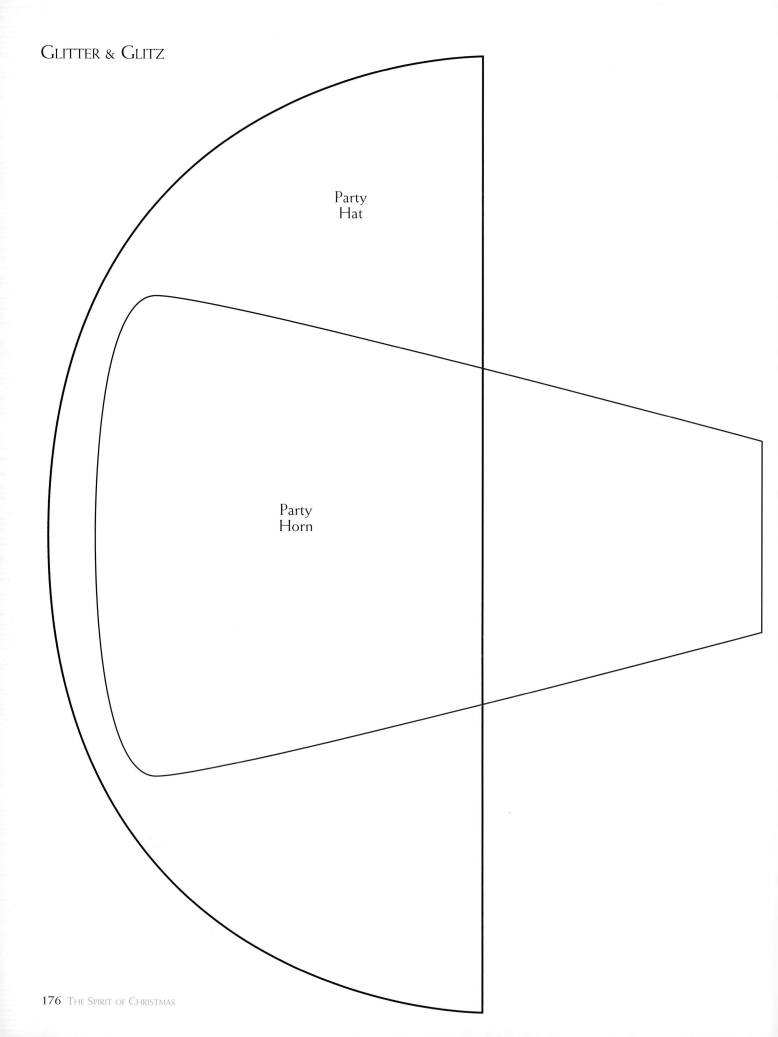

Party
Hat

Party
Horn

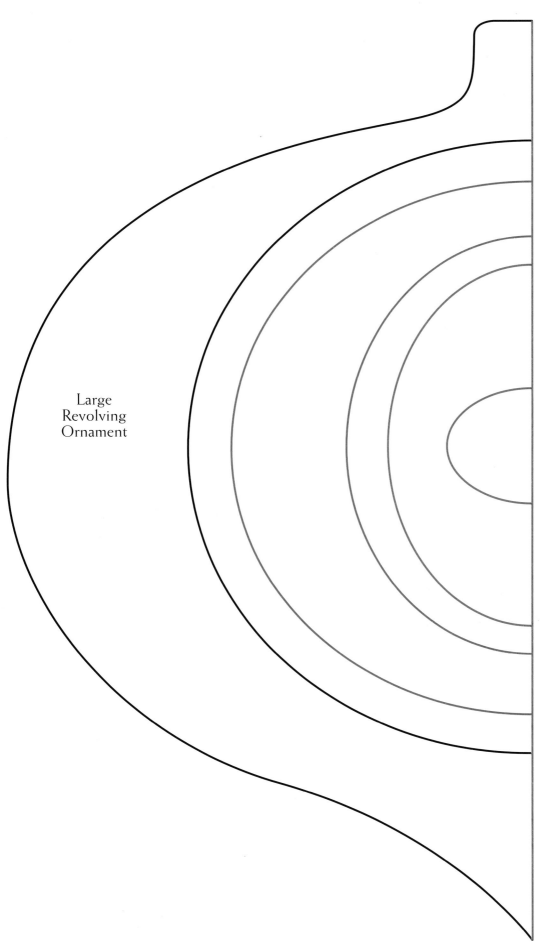

Large
Revolving
Ornament

GLITTER & GLITZ

CELEBRATING
20 YEARS OF SIGHTS
Keepsake Ornament

GLITTER & GLITZ
Invitation

Glittered Stars

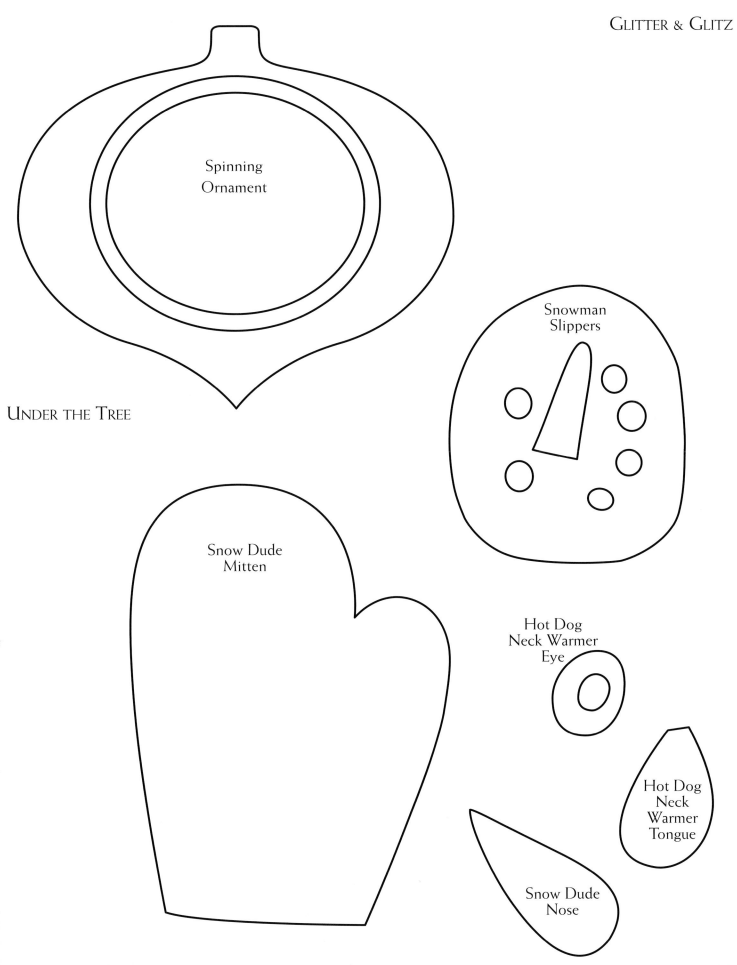

Spinning
Ornament

UNDER THE TREE

Snowman
Slippers

Snow Dude
Mitten

Hot Dog
Neck Warmer
Eye

Hot Dog
Neck
Warmer
Tongue

Snow Dude
Nose

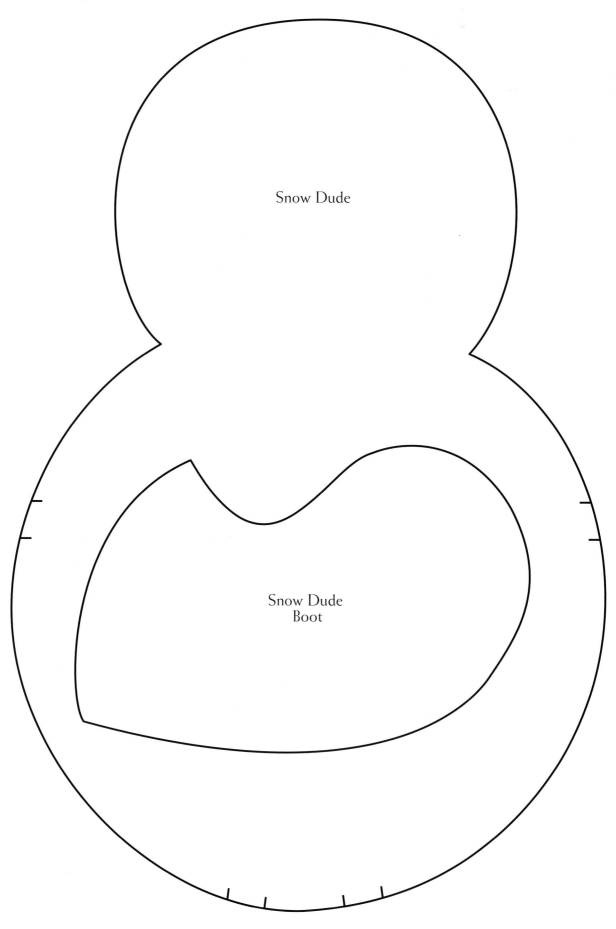

Snow Dude

Snow Dude
Boot

Holiday Box

Holiday Box

Biscuit Mix
Canister

Pound Cake
Loafpans

Pound Cake
Loafpans

Decorated
Nut Can

Popcorn
Pail

Popcorn
Pail

Candy Clipboards

Golden North Pole Nuggets

1 Package (10 oz.) peanut butter morsels
2 tbsp shortening
1 1/2 cups thin pretzel sticks
1 package (6 oz) plain fish-shaped crackers

Combine peanut butter morsels and shortening in a large glass bowl; microwave at HIGH 2 to 2 1/2 minutes, stirring once. Stir in pretzel sticks and crackers.
Drop mixture by tablespoonfuls onto wax paper.
Let stand 30 minutes or until firm. Store in an airtight container.
Yield: 2 dozen nuggets

Peppermint Candy Cups

12 ounces vanilla-flavored candy coating
3/4 cup crushed hard peppermint candy

Place candy coating in a 2-quart glass bowl; microwave at MEDIUM (50% power) 3 to 4 minutes or until melted, stirring after 2 minutes. Stir in candy. Spoon mixture evenly into petit four paper cups, filling 3/4 full. Chill until firm. Store in an airtight container.
Yield: 3 dozen candies

general INSTRUCTIONS

MAKING PATTERNS

HALF PATTERNS

When only half a pattern is shown (indicated by a solid blue line on the pattern), fold tracing paper in half. Place the fold along the blue line and trace the pattern half. Turn the folded paper over and draw over the traced lines on the remaining side of the paper to form a whole pattern.

Or, fold cardstock or fabric in half. Trace the pattern half onto tracing paper. Place the "blue line" of the pattern along the fold in the cardstock or fabric and pin or tape together outside pattern lines. Cutting through both layers, cut along the black line(s) of the pattern to cut out a whole pattern.

TRANSFERRING PATTERNS

Note: If transferring pattern onto a dark surface, use a light-colored transfer paper to transfer pattern.

Trace pattern onto tracing paper. Using removable tape, tape tracing paper pattern to project. Place transfer paper (or graphite paper), coated side down, between project and tracing paper. Use a stylus or pencil to lightly draw over pattern lines onto project.

BEADING BASICS

LOCKING BEAD

A locking bead at the beginning of a strand keeps the beads from sliding off the thread. Leaving a 3" tail, string the first bead on the thread. Pass the needle around and through the bead again to lock it. Locking beads are also used at the end of a thread or dangle.

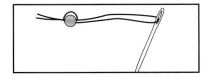

SECURING THREAD ENDS

To secure a thread end, lock the last bead and double back through the last four beads; unthread the needle, leaving a tail. Add a new thread to continue the strand (see below), or trim the tail and dot the locking bead and thread end with fray preventative; allow to dry.

ADDING THREADS

To add a thread, pass the newly threaded needle through the last three beads on the strand, leaving a 3" tail. Thread the needle through the last bead twice to lock it and continue beading. Trim the tails and dot the locking bead and thread ends with fray preventative; allow to dry.

EMBROIDERY

Follow the Stitch Diagrams to bring the needle up at odd numbers and down at even numbers.

BACKSTITCH

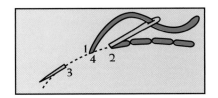

BLANKET STITCH

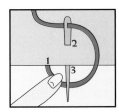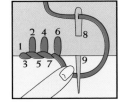

FRENCH KNOT

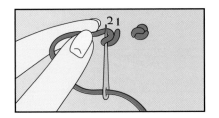

LAZY DAISY

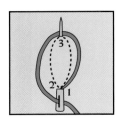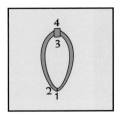

RUNNING STITCH

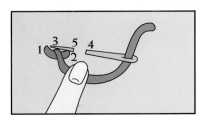

STEM STITCH

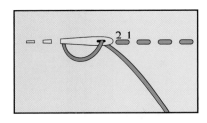

STRAIGHT STITCH

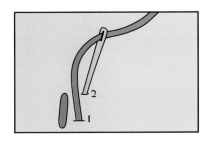

WHIPSTITCH

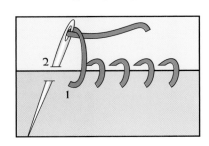

CUTTING A FABRIC CIRCLE

1. Cut a square of fabric the size indicated in the project instructions.

2. Matching right sides, fold the fabric square in half from the top to the bottom and again from the left to the right.

3. Tie one end of a length of string to a pencil. Measuring from the pencil, insert the thumbtack through the string at the length indicated in the project instructions. Insert the thumbtack through the folded corner of the fabric. Holding the tack in place and keeping the string taut, mark the cutting line (Fig. 1).

Fig. 1

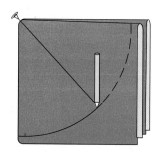

KNIT AND CROCHET

ch(s)	chain(s)
cm	centimeters
dc	double crochet(s)
hdc	half double crochet(s)
K	knit
mm	millimeters
P	purl
PSSO	pass slipped stitch over
Rnd(s)	Round(s)
sc	single crochet(s)
sl st	slip stitch
sp(s)	space(s)
SSK	slip, slip, knit
st(s)	stitch(es)
tog	together
WYF	with yarn forward
YO	yarn over

★ — work instructions following ★ as many **more** times as indicated in addition to the first time.

( ) or [ ] — work enclosed instructions **as many** times as specified by the number immediately following **or** work all enclosed instructions in the stitch or space indicated **or** contains explanatory remarks.

colon (:) — the number(s) given after a colon at the end of a row or round denote(s) the number of stitches you should have on that row or round.

GAUGE

Correct gauge is essential for proper size. Before beginning the project, make the sample swatch given in the project instructions in the yarn and hook or needle specified. Measure it, counting your stitches and rows or rounds carefully. If the swatch is the wrong size, make another one, changing the hook or needle size to get the correct gauge. Keep trying until you find the size that matches the specified gauge.

BACK LOOP ONLY

Work only in the loop(s) indicated by the arrow.

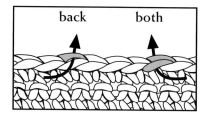

FRINGE

Cut twenty 10" lengths of yarn. Holding two strands together, fold in half. With wrong side of scarf facing and using a crochet hook, draw the folded end up through a space and pull the loose ends through the folded end (*Fig. A*); draw the knot up tightly (*Fig. B*). Repeat to fringe both ends of scarf. Trim the yarn ends.

Fig. A   **Fig. B**

INCREASES

Work the next stitch but do **not** slip the old stitch off the left needle. Insert the right needle into the **back** loop of the **same** stitch from **back** to **front** and work it. Slip the old stitch off the left needle.

KNIT 2 TOGETHER (*K2 tog*)

Insert the right needle into the **front** of the first two stitches on the left needle as if to **knit** (*Fig. 1*); then, **knit** them together as if they were one stitch.

Fig. 1

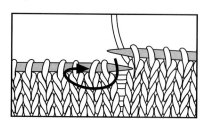

PURL 2 TOGETHER (*P2 tog*)

Insert the right needle into the **front** of the first two stitches on the left needle as if to **purl** (*Fig. 2*); then, **purl** them together as if they were one stitch.

Fig. 2

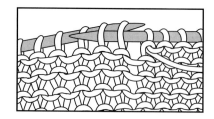

Slip, Slip, Knit (SSK)

With yarn in back of work, separately slip two stitches as if to **knit** (*Fig. 3a*). Insert the left needle into the **front** of both slipped stitches (*Fig. 3b*) and **knit** them together (*Fig. 3c*).

Fig. 3a

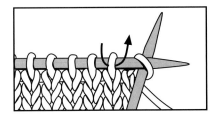

Fig. 3b

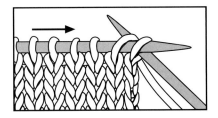

Fig. 3c

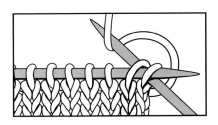

Slip 1, Knit 1, Pass Slipped Stitch Over (slip 1, K1, PSSO)

Slip one stitch as if to **knit** (*Fig. 4a*). Knit the next stitch. With the left needle, bring the slipped stitch over the knit stitch (*Fig. 4b*) and off the needle.

Fig. 4a   **Fig. 4b**

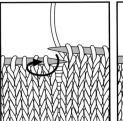 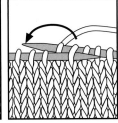

Slip 1, Knit 2 Together, Pass Slipped Stitch Over (slip 1, K2 tog, PSSO)

Slip one stitch as if to **knit** (*Fig. 5a*); then, knit the next two stitches together. With the left needle, bring the slipped stitch over the stitch just made (*Fig. 5b*) and off the needle.

Fig. 5a   **Fig. 5b**

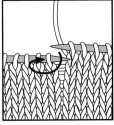 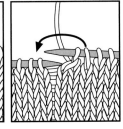

Picking Up Stitches

When instructed to pick up stitches, insert the needle from the **front** to the **back** under two strands at the edge of the worked piece (*Fig. 6*). Put the yarn around the needle as if to **knit**; then, bring the needle with the yarn back through the stitch to the right side, resulting in a stitch on the needle. Repeat this along the edge, picking up the required number of stitches. A crochet hook may be helpful to pull yarn through.

Fig. 6

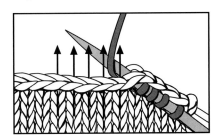

Picking Up Stitches (Purlwise)

When instructed to pick up stitches, insert the needle from the **back** to the **front** under two strands at the edge of the worked piece (*Fig. 7*). Put the yarn around the needle as if to **purl**; then, bring the needle with the yarn back through the stitch to the right side, resulting in a stitch on the needle. Repeat this along the edge, picking up the required number of stitches. A crochet hook may be helpful to pull yarn through.

Fig. 7

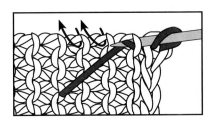

Weaving Seams

With the **right** side of both pieces facing you and edges even, sew through both sides once to secure the seam. Insert the needle under the bar **between** the first and second stitches on the row and pull the yarn through (*Fig. 8*). Insert the needle under the next bar on the second side. Repeat from side to side, being careful to match rows. If the edges are different lengths, it may be necessary to insert the needle under two bars at one edge.

Fig. 8

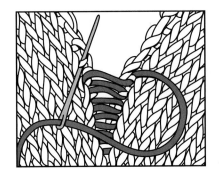

Twisted Cord

Cut 2 pieces of yarn, each 3 times as long as the desired finished length. Holding both pieces together, fasten one end to a stationary object; twist until tight. Fold in half and let it twist itself, knot both ends and cut the loops on the folded end.

project INDEX

A-B

ACCESSORIES:
Beaded Necklace & Earrings, 73
Hot Dog Neck Warmer, 73
Snowman Slippers, 71
Baking Mix Canister, 81
Baskets of Gifts, 40
Bead Garland, 59
Beaded Necklace & Earrings, 73
Beribboned Ornament, 7
Bottle Cap Garland, 50
Button Pillow, 25

C-D

CANDLES & CANDLE HOLDERS:
Etched Candle Holders, 58
Shell Candles, 38
Striped Candles, 67
Wrapped Candle Holder, 37
Candy Clipboards, 76
Cascade, 43
CENTERPIECES & TABLE DÉCOR:
Crewel Topper, 28
Dotted Bowl, 35
Embossed Velvet Table Runner, 58
Footed Bowl, 35
Glass Centerpiece, 39
Message in a Bottle, 45
Napkins, 65
Paper Tree Arrangement, 35
Papier-Mâché Platter, 35
Rose Arrangement, 28
Serving Tray, 45
Sparkly Centerpiece, 64
Table Banners, 61
Table Runner, 39
Table Skirt, 28
Champagne Flute Charms, 65
Chargers, 65
Cool Yule Cookie Bags, 77
Crewel Cropped Stockings, 25
Crewel Pillow, 25
Crewel Topper, 28
Crewel Tree Skirt, 26
Crocheted Angel, 8
Crocheted Snowflake, 9
Cupcake Picks and Wrap-Arounds, 78
Decorated Nut Can, 79

DECORATIVE ACCENTS:
Cascade, 43
Champagne Flute Charms, 65
Chargers, 65
Dotted Bowl, 35
Footed Bowl, 35
Framed Angels, 55 and 57
Framed Pieces, 29
Hanging Basket Arrangement, 25
Hanging Stars, 64
Holiday Box, 70
Large Revolving Ornaments, 64
Mantel Packages, 47
No-Melt Snowballs, 35
Painted Christmas Trees, 47
Papier-Mâché Platter, 35
Party Crackers, 66
Party Hats, 62
Party Horns, 66
Rose Arrangement, 28
Snow Dude, 71
Snow Fellow, 35
Standing Packages, 51
Tag Advent Calendar, 44
Whimsical Santa, 48
Wind Chimes, 42
Dotted Bowl, 35
Dotted Snowy Ornaments, 50

E-F

Embellished Pillow, 38
Embossed Leaf Ornaments, 59
Embossed Snowflake Ornaments, 59
Embossed Velvet Table Runner, 58
Embroidered Bird Ornament, 8
Etched Candle Holders, 58
Etched Ornaments, 59
Finger Chain Garland, 32
Flocked and Matte Red Glass Balls, 27
Folk-Art Appliquéd Ornament, 9
Footed Bowl, 35
Framed Angels, 55 and 57
Framed Ornaments, 27
Framed Pieces, 29
Frosted Ball with Beaded Collar, 7

G-K

GARLANDS & SWAGS:
Bead Garland, 59
Bottle Cap Garland, 50
Finger Chain Garland, 32
Glittered Garland, 26
Glittered Swag, 24
Seaside Swag, 41
Shell Garland, 42
Snowflake Garland, 32
Stamped Twill Garland, 32
GIFT PACKAGING, TAGS, & CARDS:
Baking Mix Canister, 81
Baskets of Gifts, 40
Candy Clipboards, 76
Cool Yule Cookie Bags, 77
Cupcake Picks and Wrap-Arounds, 78
Decorated Nut Can, 79
Icy Wrapped Packages, 56 and 57
Invitations, 60
Layered Packages, 27
Photo CD Party Favors, 66
Popcorn Pail, 80
Pound Cake Loafpans, 78
Sauce Jar, 79
Seasoning Sack, 80
Syrup Container, 77
Tag Ornaments, 41
Glass Centerpiece, 39
Glittered and Flocked Balls, 63
Glittered Garland, 26
Glittered Star Ornaments, 62
Glittered Star Toppers, 62
Glittered Swag, 24
Glittery Snowflakes, 32 and 33
Glory to God, 10
Hanging Basket Arrangement, 25
Hanging Stars, 64
Hanging Tin Star, 10
Holiday Box, 70
Hot Dog Neck Warmer, 73
Icy Wrapped Packages, 56 and 57
Invitations, 60
Joy Redwork Ornament, 8
Keepsake Ornament, 6
Knit Pillow, 38
Knit Stocking, 72
Knit Throw, 38

L-O

Large Revolving Ornaments, 64
Layered Packages, 27
Love Pillow Ornament, 8
Madonna and Child, 9
Mantel Packages, 47
Message in a Bottle, 45
Message in a Bottle Ornaments, 42
Napkins, 65
New Year Ornaments, 63
No-Melt Snowballs, 35
Ornaments with Knit Collars, 50

P-S

Painted Canvas Ornaments, 50
Painted Christmas Trees, 47
Painted Jingle Bells, 43
Painted Tree Skirt, 49
Paper Tree Arrangement, 35
Papier-Mâché Platter, 35
Papier-Mâché Snowballs, 32
Penguin, 10
Party Crackers, 66
Party Hats, 62
Party Horns, 66
Photo CD Party Favors, 66
PILLOWS & THROWS:
    Button Pillow, 25
    Crewel Pillow, 25
    Embellished Pillow, 38
    Knit Pillow, 38
    Knit Throw, 38
    Ribbon Pillow, 29
Poinsettia Angel, 9
Popcorn Pail, 80
Pound Cake Loafpans, 78
Ribbon Pillow, 29
Rose Arrangement, 28
Santa Door Hanger, 11
Santa Ornament, 10
Sauce Jar, 79
Scherenschnitte Reindeer, 11
Scherenschnitte Tree, 11
Seaside Swag, 41
Seasoning Sack, 80
Serving Tray, 45
Shell Candles, 38
Shell Garland, 42
Silver Leaf Frames, 57
Skinny Dotted Knit Stocking, 49

Skinny Striped Knit Stocking, 49
Snow Dude, 71
Snow Fellow, 35
Snowflake Garland, 32
Snowflake Pillow Ornament, 7
Snowflake Stockings, 54 and 55
Snowflake Tree Skirt, 56
Snowflake Tree Topper, 32
Snowman Ornaments, 33
Snowman Slippers, 71
Sparkly Centerpiece, 64
Spinning Ornaments, 63
Stamped Snowflake Spangles, 33
Stamped Twill Garland, 32
Standing Packages, 51
Star Tree Topper, 50
Starfish Ornaments, 42
Striped Candles, 67
STOCKINGS:
    Crewel Cropped Stockings, 25
    Knit Stocking, 72
    Skinny Dotted Knit Stocking, 49
    Skinny Striped Knit Stocking, 49
    Snowflake Stockings, 54 and 55
Syrup Container, 77

T-W

Table Banners, 61
Table Runner, 39
Table Skirt, 28
Tag Advent Calendar, 44
Tag Ornaments, 41
TECHNIQUES & TIPS:
    Beading Basics, 185
    Cutting a Fabric Circle, 186
    Embroidery, 185
    Knit and Crochet, 186
    Making Patterns, 185
    Transferring Patterns, 185
Tin Star Ornaments, 32
**TREE TRIMS, SKIRTS, &
TOPPERS:**
    Beribboned Ornament, 7
    Crewel Tree Skirt, 26
    Crocheted Angel, 8
    Crocheted Snowflake, 9
    Dotted Snowy Ornaments, 50
    Embossed Leaf Ornaments, 59
    Embossed Snowflake Ornaments, 59
    Embroidered Bird Ornament, 8
    Etched Ornaments, 59

Flocked and Matte Red Glass
    Balls, 27
Folk-Art Appliquéd Ornament, 9
Framed Angels, 55 and 57
Framed Ornaments, 27
Frosted Ball with Beaded Collar, 7
Glittered and Flocked Balls, 63
Glittered Star Ornaments, 62
Glittered Star Toppers, 62
Glittery Snowflakes, 32 and 33
Glory to God, 10
Hanging Tin Star, 10
Joy Redwork Ornament, 8
Keepsake Ornament, 6
Love Pillow Ornament, 8
Madonna and Child, 9
Message in a Bottle Ornaments, 42
New Year Ornaments, 63
Ornaments with Knit Collars, 50
Painted Canvas Ornaments, 50
Painted Jingle Bells, 43
Painted Tree Skirt, 49
Papier-Mâché Snowballs, 32
Party Hats, 62
Penguin, 10
Poinsettia Angel, 9
Santa Door Hanger, 11
Santa Ornament, 10
Scherenschnitte Reindeer, 11
Scherenschnitte Tree, 11
Silver Leaf Frames, 57
Snowflake Pillow Ornament, 7
Snowflake Tree Skirt, 56
Snowflake Tree Topper, 32
Snowman Ornaments, 33
Spinning Ornaments, 63
Stamped Snowflake Spangles, 33
Star Tree Topper, 50
Starfish Ornaments, 42
Tag Ornaments, 41
Tin Star Ornaments, 32
Wood Burned Star, 7
Whimsical Santa, 48
Wind Chimes, 42
Wood Burned Star, 7
Wrapped Candle Holder, 37

recipe INDEX

A-B

Ambrosia, 96
Ambrosia Punch, 150
APPETIZERS & SNACKS:
  Artichoke-Stuffed Mushrooms, 151
  Bacon-Cheese Ring, 18
  Black Bean Salsa, 151
  Black Bean Tartlets, 150
  Buffet Burgers, 19
  Chocolate Sugarplum Cheese
    Ball, 86
  Crazy Mixed-up Popcorn, 80
  Grilled Shrimp with Bacon and
    Jalapeños, 110
  Jalapeño Nuts, 79
  Mini Pork Sandwiches, 152
  Polynesian Meatballs, 16
  Rosemary Pecans, 150
  Savory Cocktail Tree, 151
  Slow-Cooker Queso Blanco, 113
  Sugar-and-Spice Pecans, 15
Apple and Squash Soup, 86
Artichoke-Stuffed Mushrooms, 151
Bacon-Cheese Ring, 18
BEVERAGES:
  Ambrosia Punch, 150
  Champagne Punch, 150
  Coffee-Kahlúa Punch, 106
  Fireside Coffee, 114
  Freezer Margaritas, 19
  Hot Spiced Fruit Punch, 110
  Mocha Latte, 77
  Poinsettia Sippers, 107
  Zingy Herb Tea Cider, 110
Black and White Cheesecake, 103
Black Bean Salsa, 151
Black Bean Tartlets, 150
**BREADS, BISCUITS, MUFFINS,
& PANCAKES:**
  Fennel and Coarse Salt
    Breadsticks, 89
  Jalapeño Cornbread, 111
  Quick-Mix Banana-Nut Muffins, 81
  Quick-Mix Biscuits, 81
  Quick-Mix Pancakes, 81
  Super Dinner Rolls, 97
Brownie-Mint Pie, 14
Buffet Burgers, 19

C

CAKES & CHEESECAKES:
  Black and White Cheesecake, 103
  Chocolate Espresso Cheesecake, 13
  Christmas Cupcakes, 78
  Fresh Apple and Orange Cake, 15
  Little Cherry Pound Cakes, 78
  Mocha Torte, 115
  Red Velvet Peppermint Cake, 102
CANDIES & CONFECTIONS:
  Classic Divinity, 99
  Golden North Pole Nuggets, 76
  Merry Cherry Fudge, 105
  Peppermint Candy Cups, 76
Caramel-Almond Tartlets, 106
Caramel Graham Crackers, 16
Champagne Punch, 150
Cherry Glaze, 79
Chipotle Potato Gratin, 113
Chocolate and Peanut Gelato Pie, 91
Chocolate-Caramel Thumbprints, 13
Chocolate Crème Brûlée, 14
Chocolate Espresso Cheesecake, 13
Chocolate-Mint Filling, 152
Chocolate Sugarplum Cheese Ball, 86
Christmas Cupcakes, 78
Classic Divinity, 99
Coffee-Kahlúa Punch, 106
CONDIMENTS:
  Honey Barbecue Sauce, 79
  Mocha Latte Syrup, 77
  Tex-Mex Seasoning, 80
COOKIES & BARS:
  Caramel Graham Crackers, 16
  Chocolate-Caramel
    Thumbprints, 13
  Cranberry-Streusel Bars, 102
  Crispy Pecan Sticks, 105
  Jumbo Chocolate Chip Cookies, 77
  Rudolph's Cookies, 104
  Rum Balls, 106
Cranberry-Streusel Bars, 102
Crazy Mixed-up Popcorn, 80
Cream of Turkey and Rice Soup, 98
Cream Puffs with Chocolate-Mint
  Filling, 152
Crispy Pecan Sticks, 105
Custard, 107

D-F

DESSERTS:
  Chocolate Crème Brûlée, 14
  Cream Puffs with Chocolate-Mint
    Filling, 152
  Custard, 107
  Gingerbread Trifle, 107
  Lemon Fondue, 152
  Pineapple Flan, 114
  Raspberry-Orange Bavarian
    Cream, 91
DRY MIXES:
  Quick Baking Mix, 81
  Tex-Mex Seasoning, 80
ENTRÉES:
  Mesquite-Smoked Pork with Texas
    Caviar, 113
  Mexican Rolled Meat Loaf, 19
  Parmesan Encrusted Salmon
    Fillets, 88
  Roast Turkey with Thyme Butter
    and Shallots, 94
Fennel and Coarse Salt Breadsticks, 89
Fireside Coffee, 114
Freezer Margaritas, 19
Fresh Apple and Orange Cake, 15
**FROSTINGS, GLAZE,
& FILLING:**
  Cherry Glaze, 79
  Chocolate-Mint Filling, 152
  Mocha Frosting, 115
  Peppermint Cream Cheese
    Frosting, 102

G-K

Gingerbread Trifle, 107
Golden North Pole Nuggets, 76
Green Beans with Almonds, 89
Grilled Marinated Vegetables, 112
Grilled Shrimp with Bacon and
    Jalapeños, 110
Hearts of Romaine with Cranberry
    Vinaigrette, 86
Honey Barbecue Sauce, 79
Hot Spiced Fruit Punch, 110
Jalapeño Cornbread, 111
Jalapeño Nuts, 79
Jumbo Chocolate Chip Cookies, 77
Key Lime Beurre Blanc, 88

L-O

Last-Minute Gravy, 95
Lemon Fondue, 152
Lime Soup, 111
Little Cherry Pound Cakes, 78
Merry Cherry Fudge, 105
Mesquite-Smoked Pork with Texas
    Caviar, 113
Mexican Rolled Meat Loaf, 19
Mini Pork Sandwiches, 152
Mocha Frosting, 115
Mocha Latte, 77
Mocha Latte Syrup, 77
Mocha Torte, 115
Old-Fashioned Cornbread
    Dressing, 94
Onion Casserole, 18

P-R

Parmesan Encrusted Salmon Fillets, 88
Peppermint Candy Cups, 76
Peppermint Cream Cheese
    Frosting, 102
PIES & PASTRIES:
    Brownie-Mint Pie, 14
    Caramel-Almond Tartlets, 106
    Chocolate and Peanut Gelato
        Pie, 91
    Pumpkin Chess Pie, 104
    Sweet or Savory Pastries, 17
Pineapple Flan, 114
Poinsettia Sippers, 107
Polynesian Meatballs, 16
Praline Sauce, 104
Pumpkin Chess Pie, 104
Quick Baking Mix, 81
Quick-Mix Banana-Nut Muffins, 81
Quick-Mix Biscuits, 81
Quick-Mix Pancakes, 81
Raspberry-Orange Bavarian Cream, 91
Red Velvet Peppermint Cake, 102
Rice and Fruit Dressing, 89
Roast Turkey with Thyme Butter and
    Shallots, 94
Rosemary Pecans, 150
Rudolph's Cookies, 104
Rum Balls, 106

S

SALADS & SALAD DRESSING:
    Ambrosia, 96
    Hearts of Romaine with Cranberry
        Vinaigrette, 86
SAUCES:
    Honey Barbecue Sauce, 79
    Key Lime Beurre Blanc, 88
    Last-Minute Gravy, 95
    Praline Sauce, 104
Savory Cocktail Tree, 151
Sherried Fruit Cobbler, 16
Slow-Cooker Queso Blanco, 113
SOUPS:
    Apple and Squash Soup, 86
    Cream of Turkey and Rice Soup, 98
    Lime Soup, 111
Sugar-and-Spice Pecans, 15
Super Dinner Rolls, 97
Sweet or Savory Pastries, 17

T-Z

Tex-Mex Seasoning, 80
VEGETABLES & SIDE DISHES:
    Chipotle Potato Gratin, 113
    Green Beans with Almonds, 89
    Grilled Marinated Vegetables, 112
    Old-Fashioned Cornbread
        Dressing, 94
    Onion Casserole, 18
    Rice and Fruit Dressing, 89
    Sherried Fruit Cobbler, 16
Zingy Herb Tea Cider, 110

CREDITS

We want to extend a warm thank you to the generous people who allowed us to photograph our projects at their homes.

- *It's a Wonderful Life:* Bill and Nancy Appleton
- *Snow News:* Beth and Mark Mathews
- *A Beach House Christmas, Whimsical Christmas,* and *Icy Splendor:* Mr. and Mrs. Bill Young
- *Glitter & Glitz:* Todd Crockett
- *Dinner at the Mansion:* The State of Arkansas, Governor Mike Huckabee and Janet Huckabee
- *Southwestern Grill Out:* Andrea and Brandon Keeton

For the delicious recipes and genuine hospitality that made *Dinner at the Mansion* possible, we would like to thank Arkansas Governor's Mansion Administrator Don Bingham, CEC, AAC. Special thanks also go to Chef Jason Knapp, CC, for his recipe, Green Beans with Almonds, and to Mansion Administrative Assistant Wendy Dooley for her skillful coordination.

Our sincere appreciation goes to Jerry Davis Photography, Mark Mathews Photography, and Ken West Photography, all of Little Rock, Arkansas, for their excellent work. The photo of Arkansas Governor's Mansion, page 84, is courtesy of Curt Jordan.

To JoAnn Bowling and Dale Potter we extend a special word of thanks for knitting several projects used in this book. And we are greatly appreciative of Theresa Dyke Bickley for the use of her Crocheted Angel design. Our thanks also go to Carole Prior for the lovely Knit Throw design. The delicious Fresh Apple and Orange Cake recipe is courtesy of Nora Faye Taylor, while the recipe for Chocolate Crème Brûlée was provided by Louis Petit, former owner of the Maison Louis restaurant.

We would like to recognize Royal Langnickel for the paintbrushes used on all painted designs. Mica flakes are provided courtesy of USArtQuest, Inc. of Grass Lake, MI. Soft Flock® fibers and adhesive are provided by DonJer Products Corporation of Winnebago, IL. Vellum quotes and clear adhesive monograms are courtesy of Die Cuts with a View of Provo, UT. The acrylic paints used in this book are provided by Delta Technical Coatings, Inc., of Whittier, CA. Nordic® fleece is courtesy of David Textiles, Inc. And for the many fine yarns used to create our knit and crochet projects, we thank Lion Brand Yarn Company, Coats & Clark, and Spinrite.